7-5-72

Missionary Story Sketches
Folk-Lore from Africa

KIE TIPOOR, KING OF THE BASSA-GIBI TRIBE,
OF INLAND LIBERIA.

He heartily invites and anxiously awaits the missionary with the gospel and Christian education.

Missionary Story Sketches Folk-Lore from Africa

By

ALEXANDER PRIESTLEY CAMPHOR

With an
INTRODUCTION
BY
The Rev. M. C. B. MASON

"*Let light break into the wilderness beyond you, so dense and dark with sin, and the money will come. For years the cry has come to us to put out from the shore.*"

The Black Heritage Library Collection

 BOOKS FOR LIBRARIES PRESS
FREEPORT, NEW YORK
1971

First Published 1909
Reprinted 1971

Reprinted from a copy in the
Fisk University Library Negro Collection

INTERNATIONAL STANDARD BOOK NUMBER:
0-8369-8915-5

LIBRARY OF CONGRESS CATALOG CARD NUMBER:
79-173603

PRINTED IN THE UNITED STATES OF AMERICA
BY
NEW WORLD BOOK MANUFACTURING CO., INC.
HALLANDALE, FLORIDA 33009

1701173

To

MY WIFE

INSEPARABLE PARTNER AND
HELPFUL COMPANION IN
THE VARIED EXPERI-
ENCES OF MISSION-
ARY ACTIVITIES
IN AFRICA.

These story sketches, folk-lore, and incidents reveal something of the African as he is by nature in his native habitat, and what influence the Missionary is exerting upon him in his moral and spiritual awakening. This collection has been made possible only by long and intimate touch with Africa and personal contact with native life and thought through missionary labor among them. Several of these stories first appeared in the Christian Advocate. It is the hope of the Author that the circulation of this volume, which we modestly offer to the public, may help the cause of Missions in general, and stimulate a deeper and wider interest in the field here considered.

ALEXANDER P. CAMPHOR.

Central Alabama College, Birmingham, Ala., U. S. A. February, 1909.

INTRODUCTION

THE author, Dr. Alexander Priestly Camphor, whom I have known from early boyhood, has had a strange and remarkable history. Born on a sugar-farm in Louisiana, with humble though devoted parentage, he never saw a schoolhouse until he was ten years old. Both mother and father were entirely ignorant of books and letters, but, believing that there were large possibilities for their boy, loaned him to a Methodist preacher to raise and educate. At a very early age the young boy Camphor was placed in one of the Freedmen's Aid schools and began his preparation for future work. Without the aid of hereditary strength, or the re-enforcement of foreign blood in his veins—for Dr. Camphor is a pure Negro—he learned with unusual ease and finally graduated from the New Orleans University in the regular College Course at the head of his class. He had shown such strength, both in scholarship and character, that he was at once called to the Chair of Mathematics in his Alma Mater, where for four years he taught with admirable success. It was during

INTRODUCTION

this time as teacher that the obligation of educated Negroes to help save Africa was laid upon him through a suggestion of Bishop Mallalieu, then resident in New Orleans. Accordingly he assisted in the organization of the first band of "Friends of Africa" in the institution, himself becoming the first president. As a result of this action all the schools under the direction of the Freedmen's Aid Society have at least one organization of Friends of Africa, and both the organization itself and the thought which directed it have spread among schools and Young People's Societies and Churches. As the result there is today among all educated Negroes in the South an increasing interest for Africa's evangelization.

After four years of successful work in New Orleans University, Mr. Camphor entered Gammon Theological Seminary in order to better prepare himself for his life's work, and graduated from this institution also at the head of his class. Soon afterward he became pastor in Philadelphia, later in Orange, New Jersey, at which time he did post-graduate work in Columbia University and Union Theological Seminary, New York City. Immediately after the selection of Bishop Hartzell, then Corresponding Secretary of the Freedmen's Aid Society, as Bishop of Africa, he was selected, on the Bishop's nomination, by the Missionary Board as president of the College of West Africa,

INTRODUCTION

at Monrovia, Africa, where for eleven years he met with signal success. In this appointment Dr. Camphor and Mrs. Camphor, who was constantly by his side, helper and companion, became the first regularly appointed colored missionaries of the Board of Foreign Missions to Africa. It was during this period that Dr. Camphor, not satisfied with the conditions as he saw them on the coast, made several visits to the interior, and as the result writes "Missionary Story Sketches and Folk-Lore from Africa," studying the raw material as an eye-witness in the Hinterland.

The partition of Africa by the great nations of Europe, for commercial advantage, has opened the way for the Messenger of the Cross, and this old land of the sphinx and the pyramids may once more become a center of Christian influence and power. Much of this work must be done by educated Negroes of America. The Freedmen's Aid Society alone has more than a score of its graduates there, and other educational institutions at work among the Negroes in the South have also representatives there. Mr. Camphor received the degree of Doctor of Divinity from New Orleans University and Gammon Theological Seminary. He is a thorough scholar, an eloquent preacher, a splendid administrator, and is a man of the highest integrity and tenderest love.

The book will be found both entertaining and

INTRODUCTION

instructive, and will, we trust, be very largely read by the general public and also by a large number of young colored men and women, many of whom, like the author, we trust, will give themselves for the salvation and uplift of their motherland.

M. C. B. MASON.

Cincinnati, Ohio, April 19, 1909.

CONTENTS

I

MISSIONARY STORY SKETCHES

IN LIBERIA'S WILDERNESS AND BEYOND, - - 21–128

CHAPTER I

The Arrival of a Stranger at Monrovia.—He Views a Patriotic Celebration.—Tells His Purpose in the Country.—Is Given Counsel by Old Resident, - - - 21–32

CHAPTER II

Mr. Jackson Begins Journey in Hinterland of Liberia.—What He Finds at Various Towns.—His Reception in the Bassa-Gibi Country, - - - - - 33–42

CHAPTER III

"To the Bee! To the Bee!"—The Procession to the Mountain.—The Conjuring of the Spirits.—The Close of the Annual Celebration in the Cave, - - - 43–56

CHAPTER IV

Death of an Old Chieftain.—The Body Twice Buried with Great Ceremony.—Mr. Jackson is Granted an Interview with the King.—He Pleads His Cause in an Earnest Talk.—Will He Find Favor? - 57–67

CONTENTS

Chapter V

The King is Delighted by Project.—Chieftains Heartily Concur.—The King's Address.—He Confers with Liberian Government, 68–74

Chapter VI

Trials by Fire, Smoke, and Sasswood Announced.—The Accusations.—The Young Men Innocent.—They Seek Lawful Revenge.—The Torture One Young Woman Is Put To, and Her Future Life, - 75–82

Chapter VII

"The Night is Far Spent; the Day is at Hand," - - - - - - 83–89

Chapter VIII

A Walk in a Beautiful Forest, "Where Nature Speaks Ever With God."—"Rum Ketch Dem Place Far Pass Kie Tipoor." —A Covenant Sealed.—A Night's Conversation With a King in Liberia's Wilderness, and What Characteristics It Revealed, - - - - - 90–104

Chapter IX

Mr. Jackson Spends a Day Visiting the Towns and Half Towns with the King.—He Makes Observations.—What He Jotted Down at the Close of the Day by the Light of a Torch, - - - 105–116

CONTENTS

CHAPTER X

"Where Are Our Carriers?"—"They Must be Rescued!"—Man and Beast in Deadly Combat. — A Strange Occurrence. — "Safe! Safe!" - - - 117–125

CHAPTER XI

The Leave-taking.—A Letter.—A Closing Word, - - - - - - 126–128

A WEST AFRICAN IDYL, - - - - - 129
AN AFRICAN GIRL'S STORY, - - - - 140
LOST AND FOUND, - - - - - 149
"WHAT WHITE MAN MAKE IT FOR?" - - 157
WHAT BECAME OF AN AFRICAN WITCH BABY, - 163
CAUGHT IN THE SPIDER'S WEB, - - - - 171
THE REJECTED STONE, - - - - - 178
OUT OF HEATHENISM, - - - - - 183
AN AFRICAN PRODUCT, - - - - - 190
GETTING SAVED, - - - - - 202
CLASPING HANDS WITH AFRICA, - - - 212

II

MYTHS—LEGENDS—FOLK-LORE

NATIVE STORIES, - - - - - - 231
FEMBAR'S CURIOSITY, - - - - - 232
A WOMAN TRANSFORMED INTO A LEOPARD, - - 233
A MELUSINE STORY FROM THE GOLD COAST, - 235

CONTENTS

How Dispositions are Given, - - - - 239
The Difference Between Plant Life and Animal Life, - - - - - - 240
Seddee, - - - - - - - - 241
Why the Natives Do Not Wear Clothes, - 241
War With the Baboons, - - - - - 242
The Leopard and the Dog, - - - - 243
Elephant, Hippopotamus, and Tortoise, - - 245
The Tortoise and the Pig, - - - - 247
Tortoise's Creditors, - - - - - 248
The Spider and the Pweh, - - - - 249
The Foolish Sheep, - - - - - 250
The Elephant and the Goat, - - - 251
Legends Told by a Quartet of Kroo "Boys," 252
Native Parables, - - - - - 255
Some African (Liberian) Proverbs, - - - 259

III

Native Incidents and Items

1. From Social Life

Mission Warred Upon by Cannibals, - - 265
Cannibalism of Old Times in Liberia, - - 267
An Averted War, - - - - - 269
The Ferocity and Intrepidity of an African Chief, - - - - - - 271
The Constable and the Zoe-Vleng, - - - 274
A Man in the Gri-Gri Bush, - - - 276

CONTENTS

Bettie,	277
In Sticks,	278
Execution and Other Penalties,	279
Damages,	280
Heathen Sympathy,	281
As Told by David Kelly,	282
Devotion to Duty,	285
Parents Blessing Their Children,	286
Feeding Babies,	287
Significance of African Names,	288
A Kroo Funeral,	290
Death and Mourning,	292

2. From Religious Life

Difficulties in Presenting the Gospel,	295
Controversial Doctrine Among the Heathen,	297
Tired of Waiting,	300
The Attitude of Mohammedanism in West Africa,	300
Shipwreck to Faith,	302
"Gongla"—A Rascal,	304
"God Moves in a Mysterious Way,"	307
An African's Welcome	309
God a Present Help in Trouble,	310
Quæ and His Heathen Mother,	311
What Is the Greatest Thing in the World?	314
Training-School for "Devil Doctors,"	314

CONTENTS

Conversion of a "Devil Doctor,"	316
Jasper Grant's Decision,	319
The King of Kings' Family,	321
A Letter from a Christian Mandingo,	322
Visiting Native Chiefs,	325
The Outstretched Hands of Ethiopia,	328
Thou Shalt Find It After Many Days,	330
Why A Native Man Objected to Christianity,	331
A Native Christian Lad's Testimony in the Class-Meeting,	332
Specimen Letters from Native Christians, Addressed to Bishop Hartzell in 1900,	332
"Redeemed" Girls,	333
Africa's Hope Lies in Its Young People,	353
A Kroo Boy and His Canoe,	339
Land of Flowers,	340
At a Martyr's Grave in Africa,	342
A Prayer,	344

LIST OF ILLUSTRATIONS

Facing page

KIE TIPOOR, KING OF THE BASSA-GIBI TRIBE, OF INLAND LIBERIA, - - Frontispiece

LIBERIAN MOHAMMEDANS AT PRAYER AND WORSHIP WITH KORAN, ROSARY AND WOODEN BOOKS, - - - - - - - 36

GETTING READY FOR SUPPER—WINNOWING AND POUNDING RICE IN WOODEN MORTARS, - 40

A CHIEF OF THE "DEVIL DOCTORS" FRATERNITY, - - - - - - - 48

WITCH DOCTORS APPLYING LOCAL REMEDIES COMBINED WITH OCCULT POWERS ON SICK CHILD, 76

YOUNG ASPIRANTS FOR ATHLETIC HONORS, - 110

ZOE-VLENGS, OR PRECEPTRESSES OF THE GRI-GRI BUSH IN OFFICIAL COSTUME, - - - 276

GIRL MOTHER AND BABE, - - - - 286

OUR YOUNG HOPEFULS, - - - - - 336

I
MISSIONARY STORY SKETCHES

IN LIBERIA'S WILDERNESS AND BEYOND

CHAPTER I

THE ARRIVAL OF A STRANGER AT MONROVIA.—HE VIEWS A PATRIOTIC CELEBRATION.—TELLS HIS PURPOSE IN THE COUNTRY.—IS GIVEN COUNSEL BY OLD RESIDENT.

HE had just left the steamer and had passed through the Monrovia bar, which on that beautiful morning seemed calmer than ever. Having cleared the customs, he climbed laboriously the rugged ridge on which Monrovia is built, and, looking from the piazza of one of the highest buildings in the town, viewed most of the capital and the surrounding country.

"Just think of it, a December morning, and so pleasant and balmy!" spontaneously remarked the passenger to his host.

The traveler was from the United States, and had just arrived in Liberia with the intention of finding a suitable location in the interior for the establishment of an industrial mission for the aboriginal peoples of the country. He had been an ardent student of Liberia since the return of rela-

MISSIONARY STORY SKETCHES

tives to the home land, who had been missionaries to that country. From their own lips and from books he had gathered information about Liberia, and had an intelligent grasp of the situation there, which needed only to be supplemented by personal contact and further study in the field to make his knowledge complete and accurate.

He was thoroughly convinced that he had a mission to the unreached millions of Liberia's aboriginal peoples in their vast and uninvaded wilderness, and was anxious to explore the country to ascertain the practicability of the venture and to report to friends in the home land.

Expressing further his impressions of the place, he said, "I have never seen anything like it before; such a unique country, and with such beauties of nature!"

Coming, as he did, from America in the winter season, and landing in Africa at the beginning of the dry and hot season, the change was the more strikingly pronounced. It was like entering a new world, and he gazed intently about with childlike wonder and delight.

Yonder was Krootown, a native village lying on the beach, with its three hundred or more rude dwellings, and its noisy, bustling populace. To the north stood Cape Mount, rising high, as out of the sea, and forming a bold contrast with the low-lying coast land. There also in the same di-

FOLK-LORE FROM AFRICA

rection was the white and regular shore line, stretching as far as the eye could see. To the north and east were the high and healthful uplands of the interior, with their numerous pagan tribes and vast physical resources. Stockton Creek and the Mesurado River, as well as the St. Paul's, wended their way along through the country like silver threads, while to the south and west rolled the great restless ocean, out to meet the distant horizon.

Monrovia itself presented a unique appearance. It was in holiday attire, to mark the first of December, an historic occasion, recording a signal victory of the pioneer colonists over the natives in the settlement of Monrovia in 1822. Embosomed amid a variety of tropical fruit-bearing trees and other shrubbery, and merrily floating the national colors, the attractive houses paid a silent compliment to their possessors.

The town was alive with people; residents, visitors, foreigners, and natives. Soldiers arrayed in comely uniform moved hurriedly through the streets preparatory to the parade; everything was suggestive of the occasion and its significance.

The day and its ceremonies added further to the interest of the view, all of which was of novel and peculiar interest to Mr. Jackson, the late arrival. He was soon settled in good quarters for the few days preceding his prospective tour to the

MISSIONARY STORY SKETCHES

Hinterland. Many called to welcome the newcomer and to assure him that, although he was a stranger in a strange land, he was not without friends. The cordial greetings and assurances of good-will were not only due to the favor in which he was held personally, but were occasioned also by what he contemplated doing.

"I trust you are none the worse off for your long and tedious voyage to Liberia," said an elderly man, kindly, calling to pay his respects.

"O, thank you, sir!" was the courteous reply. "I am feeling very well; remarkably well. The climate seems delightful, and what a beautiful morning! I thought it would be roasting hot."

Speaking of the voyage, he said: "I had, on the whole, a good trip across, although the seas were quite heavy between Liverpool and the Canary Islands, and the steamer encountered a storm in the Bay of Biscay; but after leaving the Islands, so calm was it that the ship simply glided along, and our voyage seemed a delightful dream."

"How different coming over nowadays is, to what it was when I came over, fifty years ago, with my family in a sailing ship!" said the old resident.

"Yes; I fancy there is quite a difference. Ocean liners of to-day are objects of wonder and admiration. In construction, management, and appointment they seem perfect, lacking nothing

FOLK-LORE FROM AFRICA

necessary for the comfort and safety of passengers. Wonderful progress, indeed, since the timorous efforts of the early mariners! The ships of the Elder Dempster and Woerman Line, between England and the west coast of Africa, have improved wonderfully in the last ten years. Some friends of ours came out ten years ago, and they tell me they were three weeks from Liverpool to Monrovia—think of it!"

"When I crossed it took three *months* to make the passage, and one never knew how or when the voyage would end; but it is a fact that among all the immigrants of those earlier days there were no disasters at sea. A kind and loving Providence seemed to have guided the vessels that brought our people to these shores. It seems to have been a case of God tempering the winds to the shorn lamb. Surely He directed our little Republic, and, I believe, is guiding now as then. And so said the orator in his address to-day."

"Yes, I remember; I was profoundly interested in the speech," Mr. Jackson said, "particularly the reference made to the earlier history of the Republic. The story is one of thrilling interest. I presume you are familiar with the subject."

"O yes, very," and opening the local paper, the *Liberia and West Africa*, which contained an account of the celebration, Mr. McLain, the caller, said: "Here it is exactly as the speaker delivered it. This paper has just been issued. Allow me to read it. I never tire of thinking and reading of Matilda Newport, whose memory we cherish and revere."

And then in a clear tone he read: "Upon the arrival of Ashmun every effort, both diplomatic and military, was put forth by the colonists to protect themselves against assaults. But despite all this the little brave band was assaulted on the morning of November 11, 1822, by eight hundred natives, armed with cutlasses and war knives, but who were repulsed by thirty-five colonists, all of whom were capable of bearing arms. Aggravated by their defeat, the natives augmented their forces to nearly sixteen hundred, and increased their determination to expel the colonists from the Cape.

"On the morning of December 1, 1822, before the break of day, hundreds of armed and hostile natives swarmed about the colony and made a second attempt to exterminate the intrepid immigrants. As they made charge after charge they were resisted by the courage and valor of the few colonists, but they were so greatly outnumbered that it seemed they must be taken by the invading kings. All the fortunes and the destiny of the colony were wrapped up in the moment.

"The strongest valor was nearly faltering, and the bravest hearts surrendering captive to despair. It was at such a crisis that Matilda Newport stepped forward and, with a coal from her pipe, touched off a deserted cannon, which made such terrific noise and sent such death-dealing pangs to the invading hosts that they fled in dismay and final defeat. Matilda Newport, by her quick thought and dauntless action, not only preserved from destruction the little colonial seed destined to blossom into the Republic, but enrolled herself among the immortal spirits of the world.

"We have met to-day to pay tribute to her life and service, to render our devotion to her memory, and to take new inspiration from the magic of her name. It is well that the citizens of Liberia should assemble to-day and hear the tongue of eloquent oratory and tell the heroic deeds of Matilda Newport and her compatriots. But for the sacrifice and courage of these early patriots there would have been no colony, and perhaps no Liberia."

Pausing, the reader said: "But I must desist; I fear I tire you. I will simply leave the paper with you, so you may read for yourself. May I ask something about your plans for the Hinterland?"

"Certainly; I shall be glad to tell you, and I invite criticism. Briefly stated, my plan is to begin with the life of the native, just where it is—in its simplicity, crudeness, barbarism, if you please—and build gradually on that. It was

MISSIONARY STORY SKETCHES

Mary Kingsley who, in calling a friend's attention to the book entitled 'Black Jamaica,' contradicted the statement that those Africans who went as slaves to Jamaica were people of no culture of their own, that they were as slates or blank sheets of paper on which any man could write what he chose. Refuting that view, she affirmed that they had a culture of their own; not a perfect one, but one that could be developed and made perfect just as European culture can be worked up.

"As I have studied missionary methods and work in Africa, I think missionaries have ignored this point. They have failed to build on the life of the natives. They look upon their institutions and nationalism as a mere welter of barbarism, and without taking the time to learn what native institutions are and what native culture is, ignorantly proceed to destroy and not heed that which is deepest and most vital in native life and thought. We ought to begin with those things that concern the African most; those things which engross his thought and life, such as his huts, farms, his children, wives, cattle, his work, and material things, and from these advance step by step to a higher conception of thought and life."

With grave earnestness Mr. Jackson further added: "You remember the Savior of mankind, the greatest of teachers, in His interview with the woman of Samaria at the well of Sychar began

FOLK-LORE FROM AFRICA

simply with the water in the well, and thus paved the way for a great, deep, spiritual truth. It is a capital illustration of the inductive method— leading from the known to the unknown, from the temporal to the spiritual. From the material water with which she was familiar He prepared her mind to grasp the 'Water of Life,' which was Himself. It would seem that the method in vogue among missionaries is to reverse the order. They put the emphasis upon those foreign and superfluous abstractions which form no part of native life and thought, and hurt more than help the African. The artless native is therefore confused and embarrassed, and they fail in reaching and saving him in any large measure.

"And again," and here Mr. Jackson sprang to his feet and paced to and fro in the animation caused by the setting forth of his ideas to interested and appreciative listeners, "we ought to build on those things which the natives have worked out through the long centuries, and gradually modify, alter, and enlarge upon them as wisdom and years of experience among them dictate, and as we find it necessary. We should devote more attention to the soil; develop its infinite possibilities and, branching out from this, take up various lines of industry as already in vogue by the African, giving him the largest possible opportunity and scope for development.

MISSIONARY STORY SKETCHES

"This done, the 'poor heathen in his blindness' will be forced to see and feel the moral force and power of the gospel of industry, of service and love, demonstrated in object lessons and crystallized in living, positive, helpful examples. This will tell mightily upon them and lead to higher things. They will have then a basis to stand on. It will give a working foundation for the superstructure we wish to build.

"But, of course," continued Mr. Jackson, dropping back into his chair, but with his manner losing none of his live interest, "I am not quite ready to begin work yet. These are only my views, as I have earnestly and prayerfully studied the question. My purpose in the country now is to increase my information concerning the interior and the tribes there, and to ascertain what prospects there are for open doors, especially for an industrial mission such as I contemplate. Do you think the prospects are bright?"

Prompt and decisive came the reply: "O yes, very bright. Liberia's present ruler has a grasp upon the interior question, which wholly concerns the aboriginal population, that few of his predecessors ever have had. His policy is not only that of conciliation as regards the natives, but the incorporation of them into the body politic. He aims to obliterate the line of division between Americo-Liberians and Aborigines, and weld by

FOLK-LORE FROM AFRICA

judicious and statesmanlike administration these two classes and make a united, prosperous, and happy people. So that under his reign the sweet dove of peace spreads her snowy wings and there is good feeling in the country. Native kings and their chieftains are not only willing, but anxious, for civilization and the blessings of Christianity. And to receive these benefits they are willing to make concessions in lands and assist in erecting buildings for school and shop as well as churches, and give all the protection in their power to the right kind of missionaries among them."

"O, that is excellent news indeed!" cried Mr. Jackson, enthusiastically.

"It is very encouraging, and should greatly stimulate the promoters of the cause of Christian Missions in the country to larger and more aggressive endeavor."

Mr. Jackson's views were not lost on Mr. McLain, who listened intently and revealed his interest in a countenance that lighted up as the speaker described his plans. "Your ideas appeal strongly to me," he said. "I believe if they are put into execution and vigorously followed from year to year, they will work successfully and bear permanent fruit. But principles and views, however sound and plausible, need to be tested by practical work and experience. They need to be carried out. That is the principal thing. Liberia

MISSIONARY STORY SKETCHES

has had theorists and dreamers in abundance. She needs more plain, earnest doers—actual workers who will bring things to pass; who make good what they plan and preach. More of this class would give to the country an outlook of larger promise and hope."

"I am glad you think well of my scheme of work. Of course, there is much to learn of the country and people, and to that task I shall assiduously address myself. I would like to be classed among the doers."

And then the mutually beneficial interview closed, as each heartily thanked the other and, with a warm exchange of personal good wishes, separated.

CHAPTER II

MR. JACKSON BEGINS JOURNEY IN HINTERLAND OF LIBERIA.—WHAT HE FINDS AT VARIOUS TOWNS.—HIS RECEPTION IN THE BASSA-GIBI COUNTRY.

ONE morning three weeks later, at an early hour, Mr. Jackson began his long journey in the Hinterland of Liberia, having made extended observations in and about the coast, visiting Liberian settlements and conversing with leading citizens in them. His general course lay in a direction northeast of Monrovia. He was accompanied by several native carriers, who bore his luggage and supplies, among which were *dashes* for the kings and chieftains through whose country he had to pass.

He was attracted to that section by the favorable reports that came from it from time to time. Those regions are elevated, healthful, well watered, and fertile, and contain a class of natives superior to those living on the coast. The people are numerous and have had very little contact with civilization. This, from all accounts, Mr. Jackson believed to be a thing in their favor, as the coast civilization is more or less corrupt, and demoralizes the natives more than it uplifts them.

MISSIONARY STORY SKETCHES

The country through which he passed was of a rugged beauty. His course extended through dense forest jungles and along winding trails worn by ages of native feet, and by rills. Within fifty miles of the coast were gradual undulations of land, succeeded by conspicuous elevations and mountains running parallel with the coast. Rivers and their tributaries flowed gently over beds of sand and gravel, and, encountering huge rocks, dashed wildly down in rapids on their journey to the sea.

The steady ascent revealed many native towns and populous tribes whose customs and life were full of interest. The reports of the country were all verified as he made a brief but careful study along the way. Although the density and fastnesses of the forest, absence of roads and bridges, and the crudeness of transportation made penetration into the interior extremely difficult, Mr. Jackson with his faithful attendants forged ahead.

After many days of hard tramping, attended with extreme physical weariness, together with many other hardships, they reached a height of land, from whose summit could be viewed, stretching for miles, charming landscapes which seemed to present an ideal district for the cherished mission. From this position as a center could be seen hills, mountains, and plains lying in all directions. There were fertile valleys blooming with the exuberance of springtime, trees laden with luscious

FOLK-LORE FROM AFRICA

fruit, and lands capable of yielding all the great tropical articles of commerce: rubber, piasava, gum copal, palm oil, and kola. In the virgin forest were varieties of valuable timbers, among which were mahogany, ebony, rosewood, and camwood; and in the native clearings were ripening fields of rice, cotton, coffee, esculent roots, and oil palms. Horses and cattle roamed the plains, and herds of elephants, furnishing ivory, fed in the uplands. These, together with other game, gave exciting sport to intrepid hunters.

"This," thought Mr. Jackson, "is the place to begin the nucleus of an indigenous civilization, taking what the natives already have as a starting point, and building as wisely as possible upon that from year to year. And again," he reasoned, "the position is strategic, being midway between the coast and the farthest inland tribes, from whom the mission would draw, and whom it would chiefly influence."

The pleasing aspect of the country, as he journeyed, allured him still further inland, although he was abundantly satisfied with the location already described, which was about two hundred and fifty miles from the coast and two thousand feet above the level of the sea. Fifty miles further brought him to an interesting walled town, twenty-five hundred paces in circumference. It was well constructed, the wall being of mud, twelve feet

MISSIONARY STORY SKETCHES

high, and four feet thick. It had five gates, and as many roads leading therefrom to other towns.

The name of this town was Quanga, situated in a mountainous region, which is part of the Kong Mountains. Here he found a thrifty class of people, giving attention not only to agriculture, but also to manufacture. Extensive tracts of land were under cultivation, yielding cotton, corn, and rice, with other tropical productions. Native looms were busy spinning thousands of yards of cotton material, while work in metal, leather, wood, bark, grass, and clay bore abundant evidence of artistic taste and skill in these several lines of handicraft. The natives were not nude, but were dressed in a manner admirably suited to the climate and their simple tastes. Cotton material from their own looms served as garments for men and women.

The women delighted in personal adornment, and their vanity, like that of their sisters of more civilized countries, manifested itself in rich and costly ornaments of gold and silver, which they wore upon their bodies. Cattle of all kinds were there in large numbers, and horses, which do not thrive on the coast, were found strong and healthy and in droves. They were used in warfare and in military demonstrations. Religiously the natives had yielded to Mohammedanism; but their religion was a crude mixture of paganism and Islam. A

Liberian Mohammedans at Prayer and Worship with Koran, Rosary, and Wooden Books.

FOLK-LORE FROM AFRICA

practical, simple Christianity instead, with its civilized accompaniments, was what they sorely needed.

Having concluded his observations here, where he was kindly received and was favorably impressed, and where he held many interesting palavers with the natives, Mr. Jackson retraced his footsteps to visit the Bassa-Gibi king and his country. It was there he had set his heart on locating the mission, provided all conditions were favorable. Everything pointed to that section as the place to carry out his plans. The king of the district had heard something of Mr. Jackson's intentions and had dispatched messengers ahead, who met him in the path fifty miles from his starting point, bearing greetings from their king and urging him onward, to become, upon arrival at the capital, His Majesty's stranger.

Of course, all along the way this was known, and Mr. Jackson was greeted as the big king's stranger and was hospitably received everywhere. He repaid their hospitality by bestowing little gratuities in beads, matches, pins, needles, fish-hooks, and pieces of cotton material. Having taken a route that lay slightly in a different direction, he did not avail himself of the king's invitation on his outward journey, but now resolved to do so.

As he and his carriers emerged from a long strip of dense forest in which they had walked from sunrise to sunset, they entered wearily a well-worn serpentine path, which led to the king's own town. The short twilight had ended and it was evening by the time they reached their destination, but the light of the full moon made it almost as bright as day in the large, open clearings in which the town was located. All was hum and bustle in this heathen community. Crowds of natives, men, women, and children, had come from all points of the compass for miles away, making this a rendezvous from which to take a direct route leading to the mountain twenty miles away, where the annual sacrifice for the Gibi people was to be held.

The town presented an interesting aspect. The small rude huts of which it was composed were overcrowded, and, to provide for the large transient population, temporary booths of bamboo and palm leaves were constructed and promiscuously scattered in the groves which skirted the dense forest. Scores of towns and sub-districts were represented by deputations of chiefs and influential men. Women and children, young men and maidens, all were there to act their part in the drama which the occasion created. Food and drink were in abundance; music and dancing lent their charms to further enliven the moments and make the event memorable.

"I fear, Mr. Jackson," said his interpreter,

FOLK-LORE FROM AFRICA

"that this is not an opportune time to approach the king on the subject of missions. This is the season when the natives give themselves wholly to their fetich worship. The town, as you can see, is alive with people for that purpose. To-morrow the annual celebration takes place in the mountain. The food and animals for the offering have already been dispatched, and how long these ceremonies will last no one can tell.

"The natives neglect their homes, their farms, everything, and devote themselves to the observance of these rites. Nothing seems more important to them than these tribal laws and customs. To these they are wedded, they having been handed down to them through the centuries. They are vital to them, and it is almost impossible to direct their attention to anything else, however important."

"So I understand," answered Mr. Jackson; "but let us not despair! Let us be patient and wait a little while. Perhaps conditions may be more favorable than we anticipate."

The entrance of the stranger and his attendants to the town was not unobserved by the quick eyes of the natives, who saw them while they were yet afar off, and who bore the news of their approach to the king. And by the time they had fairly entered the town messengers from the king greeted them and they were conducted to the palaver house, a large, airy, and comfortable building thirty-six feet square, built especially for the reception of strangers. Here followed a brief and informal interview with Mr. Jackson, through his interpreter and the king's oldest son, surrounded by a group of chieftains.

As is customary when strangers of note enter a native village, gratuities or *dashes* were made to the king, as a compliment to him and expressing the good-will of the donor. They were received with thanks by the king's representatives. The object of the visit was explained, and a request was made for an interview with the king. To this came the answer that, in view of the approaching ceremonies and the many urgent duties that claimed his attention, he would be obliged to forego the pleasure of an interview until a more convenient season, when the request would receive proper and ample consideration.

In the meantime the king extended the freedom of the town and country to the strangers and requested that they should consider themselves his guests. They were assigned quarters for the night, which consisted of three conically shaped huts built of poles and daubed with clay, with thatch covering as roofing. Their entertainment was, of course, simple, yet adequate for native conditions. A mat spread on a floor of solid earth beaten hard as a rock served as a table, on which were placed large bowls of rice and smoked fish, accompanied with

GETTING READY FOR SUPPER.—WINNOWING AND POUNDING RICE IN WOODEN MORTARS.

FOLK-LORE FROM AFRICA

palm oil. These were eaten with large wooden spoons. The party drank water from the spring down at the foot of the hill, a quarter of a mile from the town.

The only change in subsequent meals was that of boiled cassava beaten into a pulp and called *dumboy*. This was substituted for rice, and served with hot soup highly seasoned with pepper and salt, and flavored with palm oil. After supper they were ready to retire for the night. The long and labored walk of the day through a dense forest without roads, ascending and descending hills and mountains, crossing rivers by wading and swimming them, and leaping from rock to rock, and other obstructions which lie in their beds, made Mr. Jackson, to whom such experiences were new, physically very weary; and the sight of a bed, though only a mound of hard-beaten clay flattened on the top, over which was spread a grass mat and a native coverlet, was most inviting. But its occupant was too exhausted to sleep, and besides, slumber was impossible where there was such confusion and uproar.

"All night it seems that those drums and horns kept up a steady noise. How tired and sore those people must be!" said Mr. Jackson, as he arose the next morning and looked upon the moving crowd without through the large cracks which freely admitted the light in the little thatch hut.

MISSIONARY STORY SKETCHES

They were still in motion under the magic spell of the musicians and dancers, and were in gleeful spirits.

"Tired?" said Jarbar, surprisedly. "Never. Their physique admits of tremendous endurance, and even torture, and their fanaticism is such that they can continue such speed until they drop from exhaustion."

"But what a pity that there should be such energy, strength, and enthusiasm misdirected!" said Mr. Jackson.

"Yes, it is a sad pity," replied Jarbar, sympathetically; "but the African in his heathen life does not consider it as such. The descriptions given by Christians of his heathenism do not exist to him. It is only when lifted out of the meshes of pagan conditions and given higher ideals and broader horizons that he is able to behold the contrast and appreciate the change. He always rejoices in the transition from darkness to light."

Jarbar spoke from personal experience. He himself had been a pronounced heathen, but was now civilized, earnestly seeking to promote the good of his native brethren, to whom he felt himself debtor. He had accompanied Mr. Jackson on this long journey without any remuneration because he was deeply interested in his scheme, and believed that, if carried out, it would bring great and permanent blessings to the native population.

CHAPTER III

"To the Bee! To the Bee!"—The Procession to the Mountain.—The Conjuring of the Spirits.—The Close of the Annual Celebration in the Cave.

UNEARTHLY yells of "To the Bee! To the Bee!" uttered in the native dialects, issued from the hoarse, gutteral throats of a chorus of "devil doctors," who, with frightful grimaces and inimitable contortions of the body, led the procession frantically on to the precipitous peak of the Gibi Mountain, called the Bee, twenty miles away. They had sat for many hours during the night in solemn conclave in the sacred groves, communicating with the spirits whose mediums they were and under whose influence they acted, and had unanimously agreed to begin the performance at break of day.

They were fantastically dressed. On some of their heads they supported heavy ebony masks having two ugly faces, one before and one behind. These were artistically carved in grewsome figures, representing some weird and ancient design. A heavy dress of palm filament dyed black, bulging out as though held in place by bamboo hoops, covered the body from the waist down to the bare feet.

MISSIONARY STORY SKETCHES

A garment of native fabric covered the breast, and gaudy handkerchiefs arranged in fanciful folds played about the neck, breast, and shoulders. The slightest movement of the body was attended by a rustling noise which the dry leaves made, and the hop, skip, and sway of the body to the beat of drums and the toot of horns furnished amusing and ludicrous antics. A cloud of dust followed the movements of these mysterious personages, and at times they were completely hidden from view.

The procession emptied the town of all its inmates and moved toward the mountain like a flowing river along its course. Next to the "devil doctors" were the king and his chieftains, and in this group were other kings and chiefs from neighboring tribes. The warriors came next, and behind them, in solid phalanx, were the strong young men, following hard in the footsteps of their sires. They each bore a palm branch in their right hand, and their native songs, a sort of recitative and refrain, were more vociferous than musical. Women, old and young, were in the line and greatly outnumbered the men. The king alone claimed three hundred of these as wives, and there were other leading men who had a score or more. Children accompanied their elders and took in the picturesque scene with the aptitude peculiar to childhood.

There was no invitation extended to Mr. Jackson to accompany the procession, but neither did any one object to his doing so. The "devil doctors," however, looked askance at his carriers as they bore portions of his luggage containing his camera outfit, and were just a little disturbed at the sight of his note-book and pencil in hand. Though heavily masked, they had thoroughly scrutinized him, and felt instinctively that, though belonging to the same race and having the same dusky hue, he was nevertheless not of their ilk, and was their adversary, though apparently harmless and friendly.

"Daddy!" exclaimed one of Mr. Jackson's carriers, excitedly, "dem witch man say he no be good for you to draw people this time. He be bad for true."

He had run hurriedly through the tall grass and interlaced vines along the side of the procession from its head to the end of the line where Mr. Jackson was about to adjust his tripod to snap a view of the scene. His timely speech seemed a relief to him, for he was thoroughly in sympathy with Mr. Jackson and liked him, and was anxious that no harm befall him.

"What! I can't take a picture?" asked Mr. Jackson, revealing surprise in his tones and gestures.

"No, daddy," said the native emphatically, "not this time."

"Why?" asked Mr. Jackson, impatiently.

MISSIONARY STORY SKETCHES

"Daddy," attempting to give an explanation, "dis people, he no be all same coast people. S'pose you draw Kroo man, and Kroo woman, Kroo picaninny, he like him too much. Kroo people saby (understand) dem draw ting. Dis people he Gibi people. He no saby dat. He be scared dem camera. He say witch lib in dem small hole wid dem glass ting. He say dem witch pass he witch."

This statement of the carrier set forth the usual state of the case. Many of the chiefs and natives of the up country are very much afraid of the camera. They believe that there is something mysterious about the lens, and that if they are photographed their spirit will either leave their bodies or they will die by a lingering death.

Mr. Jackson respected the superstitious belief of the people and reluctantly ordered that the camera be put away. He further declined taking notes, as this, too, was objectionable to the witch doctors.

On the route to the mountain, about midway, is the grave of Nawvlee, one of the old and powerful kings of the Gibi people. It is marked by a huge granite rock and occupies a plot of ground enclosed by bamboo palings. Within the enclosure are placed articles of various kinds, such as broken pots, plates, pipes, bowls, jugs, beads, coral, bits of glass, chinaware, toy statuary, and an old nickel-plated clock. On the center of the grave stands a large demijohn of palm wine, a native beverage from the palm tree. These are there as marks and fitting tributes to keep alive the memory of their mighty dead. While other and unmarked graves are scattered in and about the towns and half towns, this one lies in a secluded spot away from the road side, in the forest, apart and alone, bearing abundant evidence that he who lies there is still revered by a grateful people.

"The procession is halting," cried Jarbar. "Hear the toot, toot, toot of the horns and the boom, boom, boom of the drums; it is a signal for the line to stop in order to allow the witch doctors to encircle around the grave of their long-dead king and communicate with his wandering spirit in its dark and distant abode."

"Why call him back?" said Mr. Jackson, inquiringly.

"That they may be rejuvenated by new hope and contact with his disembodied spirit, and reassured in the faith of their fetich devotions," was the thoughtful reply.

The ceremonies at the grave were in keeping with their superstitious customs, but somewhat abbreviated, to be concluded at the mountain not far away. On and on filed the thronging multitude. Before them rose in full view the conspicuous peak of the Gibi Mountain, measuring three thousand feet or more, being a part of a system or chain of mountains stretching many miles away. Between these ranges are beautiful, well-watered, and fertile valleys, constantly receiving their richness from the mountains and plateaus by which they are surrounded. The Bee is covered with luxuriant foliage, and studded with giant trees from its base to its summit. A face of bare rocks on its western slope forms an open level plot, from which may be viewed Careysburg and Monrovia to the west, the Galilee Mountains to the southwest, and the hills of Bopora to the north. At the base of this bold cliff, on its southwestern side, is a cave with two apartments of considerable width and depth.

In these dark and grewsome recesses the natives assemble for sacrifice and worship, making regular pilgrimages thereto. Near the mouth of the cave are huge rocks. The mountain with its cavern and massive stones is sacred to the Gibi people. In its fastnesses they seek refuge from invading foes and claim protection of the tutelar deity and associated spirits dwelling therein. This precipice with its craggy height renders access impossible to the enemy and furnishes a safe retreat to the troubled inhabitants.

"Softly, softly!" were the words passed down the line as the witch doctors, leading men and women neared the mouth of the cave.

"Let no one speak!" shouted Jo, the chief of the "devil doctors," as he sat on a rock command-

A Chief of the "Devil Doctors" Fraternity.

ing a view of the whole crowd. He was covered from head to foot with charms and fetiches. One of these was of especially large size and was swung from the neck and rested on the breast. This was a powerful ju-ju, and its possessor was proud of it. His associates, like him, wore charms and, in common with their leader, claimed for them tremendous power.

Conspicuous in the procession were King Kie Tipoor, Jo, Creh, Beoh, successor to King Nawvlee, the dead king at whose grave the ceremony was held; Turplah, Borpeh, Florgah, Peygebor, Somah, Furpah, Gurzatoe, Zeah, and Jay Jay Nough. Among the women were Fomi, Zown-Betti, Jo-Jonor, Taplah, Tarmah, and others. Among the younger men were Boyaryu, Tarpu, Kenkkenk, Gahlway, Butcher, and Sunu, while some of the towns represented were Kie Tipoor, Guey xa to, Zway bee, Sawyonah, Gaywaryarku, Bo, Po, Gayzu, Sawblee, Somar, Zeo, and Swar. These towns covered an area requiring four to five days' walk, as the natives travel, to reach the mountain.

Noiselessly the people trod in obedience to the commands of their guides and in keeping with an honorary custom, as they congregated at the base of the mountain. There were two apartments of immense capacity made by huge rocks whose natural position forms a cave, having a large aperture.

MISSIONARY STORY SKETCHES

The cavern is entered by a long pathway of towering and dangerous rocks extending on either side. One of the apartments tapers into a large, narrow subterranean cavity, where it is lost to view in the darkness of the cave. These gloomy recesses are the abode of innumerable vampires, whose flight and noise make the cave hideous by day and night. Attracted by the awe which the mountain and huge rocks inspire, and the dark mystery which lurks about the spot, the Gibi people in their deep need for God imagine that they find Him here. In their groping search for some higher power than themselves, they make pilgrimages and offer sacrifices in this mountain, claiming protection and achieving victories over their enemies in war.

The mountain is now reached, and along the stony pathway file the crowd, making their way to the cave.

"Crowd in!" is the order from the leader of the "devil doctors," occupying still the rocky pinnacle, from which he descends and, leading the way, enters the cave, which is quickly filled with five hundred or more eager, idolatrous worshipers. As many again, who could not enter, squatted reverently in family groups outside the cave and along the grassy slopes of the mount.

"Bring in the sacrifices!" again he utters, and the panting, blatting rams are dragged over the jagged rocks, gnarled roots, and shrubbery by strong, willing hands and placed securely in the cavities of the rocks to await the pleasure of the spirits who dwell there. A white fowl, large quantities of food and drink, are also added to complete the offering.

Now begins the conjuring of the spirits by the chorus of "devil doctors," high priests of occult mysteries, in which they are expert. Powerful and numerous fetiches are employed, and after a wearying scene of senseless mutterings and uncanny performances, which seem only an introduction to the more elaborate ceremonies to follow, they, standing erect, with face upturned to the top of the cave and speaking aloud in feeling tones, address the spirits as follows, one of their number holding the white fowl brought as an offering, and another a plate filled with rice placed near the mouth of the chicken:

"Spirits of our kings and chieftains dwelling in the cave of this mountain, we now come to meet you this day. We have left our towns and farms behind and have walked this long, rough way with our wives and children to be here. We bring you this peace offering, and beg you in the name of our king to accept it, letting us know the state of your mind by making this fowl peck the rice we place before it."

There is silence for some minutes. All eagerly await returns from the spirits, looking intently

MISSIONARY STORY SKETCHES

upon the chicken, watching to see its least quiver of movement toward the rice. But in this they are disappointed. The time drags wearily on for three hours, with no response. Then there are feverish stirs and mutterings, followed by loud, pathetic, and importunate cries, pleading with the spirits to accept the offering. Women whom the witch doctors pressed down in the dark recesses, claiming they are by nature nearer the underworld than men and are therefore nearer the spirits, are loud in their orisons.

They lay upon the ground with their faces to the earth, and plead and plead with tear-dimmed eyes, covering their bodies with self-inflicted bruises made by their frantic dashings against the rocks. The old king, conscience-smitten, fears lest the delay is due to some moral lapses or remissness of duty on his part, as the head of the tribe, and steps up in the midst of the "devil doctors" and, with outstretched arms, pleads thus with the spirits:

"Why is it you do not give us an answer? Here we are in your presence. We have been begging you all we know how for the past three hours, and yet you pay us no heed. What is the thing we have done that displeases you? Tell us. Tell us, that we may make the necessary atonement for our sins at once and return to our towns satisfied."

"The spirits will not accept the offering," an-

FOLK-LORE FROM AFRICA

grily thunders Jo, the chief of the "devil doctors," his eyes flashing fire as he speaks. He looks like a demon in human form. His countenance combines every feature that defines malignity and hate; and emboldened by the yells of approval that puncture his remarks, by his associates, he adds, "Put the strangers out of the cave!" and, as though waiting for the agreement of those who are like-minded, he adds, "If they do n't leave, I 'll throw witch on every one of them and kill them instantly."

"What is that 'devil doctor' saying?" asks Mr. Jackson of his interpreter, apprehensively. He fancies that his words were directed specially at him, and although spoken in the outlandish jargon of these bush people, he instinctively takes in their meaning and feels that he must withdraw.

"It means no good for us," replies Jarbar, evasively, who desires to spare Mr. Jackson the embarrassment of knowing what was said.

With this they all leave the cave to its rightful occupants, and withdraw to a great enough distance to satisfy the "devil doctors," and yet view the whole proceedings.

The exit of the strangers is a relief to the "devil doctors" and the rest of the people in the cave. The delay of the response from the spirits has been becoming more and more embarrassing to the leaders of the ceremony, whose fetiches are supposed to work miracles; and to be worsted in the presence of strangers is not a thing to be desired. It is not considered, under the circumstances, a discourtesy to speak thus to Mr. Jackson and his men. Nothing is permitted to interfere with fetich worship; this taking precedence of all else.

The king resumes his address, saying: "Are you displeased because of the disputes and wrangling between King Nawvlee's and Crah's children? One of the Nawvlee's sons is already dead and has gone to where you are in this cave. That can not be the cause of your silence and displeasure, can it? Are you displeased because I failed to give a big dinner to the soldiers who fought in the late ten-years' war with the Pessy tribe? Is that the reason why you refuse us now? If that is it, speak through this chicken by making it peck this rice."

The earnestness, eloquence, and pathos which this address combines, accompanied with the gestures in its delivery by this heathen king, is marvelous. As this stalwart figure moves among the people, swaying his body to and fro, trembling under deep emotion, he seems every inch a leader, although a blind and misguided one. The picture suggests a scene described in the Book of Kings, concerning the false prophets of Baal at Mount Carmel crying aloud from morning until noon, saying, "Baal, hear us!"

It is an interesting coincidence that immedi-

FOLK-LORE FROM AFRICA

ately after the departure of the strangers from the cave, and the close of the king's address, the chicken, which had remained apparently lifeless for three hours, suddenly begins to revive and flutter vigorously, and then greedily devour the rice. The excitement that follows is as the sudden bursting of a volcano. It seems as though the cave will explode under the pressure of the wild and furious yells in which all indulge. It is a tempest of heathen passion, a union of intense feeling and joy over their victory in the cave. Women and children scream hysterically, and men, old and young, shout vociferously. As an expression of admiration and gratitude to the king, he is seized and bodily lifted in the arms of his stalwart courtiers and borne amid a chorus of frenzied shouts and applause.

All is stir and life afterwards. The news spreads quickly from one to the other, and soon every soul is jubilant with the shouts of victory. The rams are quickly slaughtered, their blood poured in bowls, and the quivering flesh, with the other articles they have brought, offered as sacrifice. Then follow music and dancing, in which there is a blending of voices and instruments. Under the influence of these charms there is hilarity and a full flow of life, which continue the rest of the day and a large part of the night. The occasion is not without some bits of romance. Many

MISSIONARY STORY SKETCHES

of the young men and maidens under the spell of the irresistible and bewitching full moon stroll off in congenial groups in the groves, and there in quiet repose exchange sweet counsels of incipient love. The joy that emanated from the cave has touched responsive chords of thrilling notes.

"The mountain scene," ponders Mr. Jackson, as he threads his way back to his quarters at Kie Tipoor, "tells its own story. How far humanity may wander in the darkness of fanaticism and superstition without the light of revelation! The heathen sorely needs something better than fetiches to answer all his physical and spiritual needs. Unaided and alone he must inevitably stagger and sink to still lower depths of darkness and folly. What a challenge his moral and spiritual destitution, as revealed in this mountain scene, makes to Christendom!"

CHAPTER IV

DEATH OF AN OLD CHIEFTAIN.—THE BODY TWICE BURIED WITH GREAT CEREMONY. — MR. JACKSON IS GRANTED AN INTERVIEW WITH THE KING.—HE PLEADS HIS CAUSE IN AN EARNEST TALK.—WILL HE FIND FAVOR?

ON the morrow the mountain and the cave presented a different aspect to that of the previous day. All was stillness save the song of the birds and the wind among the branches of the trees, commingled with the sound of water falling over the rocks in the streams, making its way down the mountain sides. The people who on the day before had made the mountain a picturesque scene of life and interest, had returned to their several towns to continue the festivities during the remaining period of the full moon.

But while these were in full blast the announcement came of the death of the old chieftain at Goyduo, a neighboring town to Kie Tipoor. There was at once in all the towns near by a vigorous beating of the drums, whose taps bespoke death and heralded a summoning of the people to the palaver house, calling off the festivities of mirth, to be replaced by those of mourning. The deceased had died in the sick bush, a native hospital located in an obscure half town in the forest. The news of his death spread rapidly and was regarded as a great calamity.

The corpse was wrapped in a mat made of grass and borne laboriously along the road from the sick bush, which was a mere rough footpath that had many bends and turns. All along the path piteous wails of friends and relatives were heard. Their cries, mingling with the weird toots of horns and taps of drums, were heart-rending. Two of the devil fraternity, fleet of foot, passed excitedly through the bush near the towns, shouting in mournful strains.

"Where is he? Where is he?" they cried.

The answer was, "He is gone! He is gone!"

This was followed by another thrice-repeated query: "What has he gone for? What has he gone for? What has he gone for?"

The reply was, "To take a long walk."

Again came the query, "When is he coming back?"

"We do n't know; he did n't say," was the slow and dirge-like rejoinder.

When the body reached its destination it was swathed in a number of country cloths, laid out in a hut and smoked, and after a short period of time was buried in "half ground," that is, partly buried. There it remained until the relatives and

FOLK-LORE FROM AFRICA

friends of the deceased obtained all the means necessary to conclude the ceremonies, making them in keeping with the rank and station of the deceased. Nothing was too great a sacrifice for the honored dead.

There have been instances in the history of this people when slaves, children, and towns have been pledged to secure means to defray the expenses incurred in burying the dead.

Notice of a second burial was given, and the news spread far and near through the country. The call was heeded and the natives poured in large numbers into the town to pay their last tribute of respect to the dead chief.

On the appointed day for the final interment the unsightly remains were exhumed, dressed, and laid on a new mat. All the fetiches, charms, and ju-jus that belonged to the chief in life were placed by his side. Around him were gathered his score of wailing and almost denuded widows. Their heads were shaven and bodies sprinkled with ashes. They bore indications of poignant grief and sorrow. With these were the children and other relatives and friends, no less affected, to judge from their cries and lamentations. The singers chanted the praises of the dead, and dancers in high spirits exhibited the poetry of motion in their swaying arms and bodies and nimble feet, which kept time to the music of the horns and drums.

MISSIONARY STORY SKETCHES

Friends paid tributes of respect by their presence, and by gifts of palm oil, tobacco, rice, and more expensive things. Sympathy for the bereaved was expressed. Bullocks were slaughtered and their blood poured in basins as a libation to the spirits. Their flesh furnished a feast and offering for both the dead and the living. Rum and native beverages were plentiful and freely drunk.

To the unrestrained wails of the weeping and shouts of the merry were added long and successive volleys of guns, all of which, while deafening to the stranger, was appropriate honor for the dead and welcome sounds to the mourners. When every possible means of display was exhausted, the procession started to the grave. All that remained of the chief was borne by carriers and laid deep in the earth. The grave was in a quiet grove near the town, the spot marked by a large stone. Around it were placed many of the presents brought to the dead, including food and drink. The ceremonies were concluded with a division of the property belonging to the deceased, his widows, personal effects, all of which fell to rightful heirs according to native laws.

Mr. Jackson observed the funeral ceremonies from beginning to end. To him these performances were startling. While he had read much in books of African customs, and had talked with persons who were familiar with the subject, it was nothing to be compared with seeing these conditions in actual life for one's self. And his purpose in undertaking this long and perilous journey in the interior was that he might study the native in his original *habitat*, uninfluenced by civilization.

He was impressed by many things. The high and healthful uplands of the interior are by far superior to the lowlands of the coast. Here the climate is salubrious and the soil capable of producing in abundance all the tropical vegetation for which the continent is noted. In the bowels of the earth is mineral wealth, the limits of which are unknown. The vast forest is as a gold mine, yielding to the organized and well-directed efforts of the thrifty and intelligent a constant and productive source of supply. Its valuable timbers, trees, fibers, gums, fruits, and vines offered large scope for lucrative trade and commerce.

Indeed, every prospect was for the most part pleasing. While there were some difficulties, they were not insuperable. The people were numerous and, although living a crude, primitive, heathen life, had within them elements of promise. The brighest hope was in the young people. The young men who had visited the coast had returned with new conceptions of life. They were becoming restless and dissatisfied with the old order of things.

MISSIONARY STORY SKETCHES

They wanted something better; just what, they did not know. Fetichism was not meeting their needs as it had their fathers', and confidence in it was gradually waning. To Mr. Jackson it seemed that the time was ripe for the introduction of the principles of the gospel of Jesus Christ, with its corresponding practical benefits. This as a nucleus would spread, and offset the advance of a corrupt civilization from without and rescue the heathen from paganism about him. It would, in short, meet all his needs.

Mr. Jackson realized that there was much to be done before these ends could be accomplished. He knew that there would be many delays before he would be permitted to see even a fair beginning of his plans bear fruit. But he was hopeful, and was willing to labor patiently. He knew that results mature slowly in Africa; but when a work of the kind he contemplated once became firmly rooted it would grow and become a fixture in the soil, a perennial blessing to the people. He was now anxious to meet the paramount chief personally and hold a palaver with him on the prospects of establishing a mission in his country. The fetich ceremonies for the time being had ended, and the natives were now busy at their farms, clearing the land, burning brush, and preparing to plant cassava and their principal farm products. There was no better time than this for the interview.

FOLK-LORE FROM AFRICA

The next day at noon the long-expected summons for the interview with the king was announced. The call was made by vigorous tappings on the palaver drum and a grand flourish of native trumpets, supported by a chorus of girls discoursing music with instruments and voice. The call attracted wide attention, and Kie Tipoor, with its surrounding half towns, was not indifferent to the issues of the day. Messengers were hastily dispatched to the towns where the chieftains lived, calling them to the official quarters of the king. They responded, bringing with them groups of leading men from their respective towns. The reception was at the palaver house and was in keeping with native etiquette.

Mr. Jackson's quiet and sober demeanor had not been unnoticed by the natives, who had carefully scrutinized him, and who had found his personality impressive. Kind, generous, unselfish, and discreet, he had not failed in winning them; and the reception that awaited him was an expression of their feeling toward him, and was a display of native hospitality as beautiful as it was royal. The presents, or "dashes," as they are called, that Mr. Jackson presented to the king had had their effect in a most pleasing way, and a more formal presentation at this time, accompanied by a brief and well-worded speech, provoked smiles and stimulated good cheer for the giver and his project.

MISSIONARY STORY SKETCHES

The king, a tall and well-proportioned man of seventy, with keen and penetrating eyes, expressive of an alert mind, in bearing sober, and with manners easy and cordial, reclined in a hammock, while around him sat his chieftains, to whom are submitted matters of importance claiming the public attention. From them a unanimity of sentiment is usually required before they are considered approved or ratified. In exceptional cases the king acts without the council of his subordinate chiefs.

Mr. Jackson sat in the center of the group with his interpreter, and in a brief address stated the object of his visitation: first, to fulfill a long-cherished wish to visit the interior of Liberia northeast of Monrovia, and of forming the personal acquaintance of the kings and chiefs of those regions.

"I desire this," he said, "not for purposes of trade, but for the moral and spiritual uplift of the people, in whose welfare I am specially concerned. I am anxious to gather practical information so as to launch a project that contemplates the civilization and Christianizing of the heathen tribes in these regions hitherto unreached. This, in my judgment, can be most effectively accomplished by the establishment of an agricultural and industrial mission in your midst.

"It should be on a broad and ample basis, having the primitive industries of the nations as a starting point. From year to year there would

FOLK-LORE FROM AFRICA

be improvements. The mission would begin with a small group of native buildings—workshops, schoolhouse, chapel, dormitories, and farm. These would constitute the nucleus of an indigenous civilization which would aim to touch and improve every phase of native life, material and spiritual. Your huts would be made more permanent and sanitary; your farms more productive and varied in crops; your methods of administering to the sick and wounded more humane and scientific; your knowledge of agricultural and mechanical implements improved; simple instruction in letters imparted; moral precepts and sentiments inculcated, and the teachings of Jesus Christ as revealed in the Divine Book instilled in minds and hearts. In fact, my scheme aims to help the people in every point of their being by stimulation and improvement."

Mr. Jackson gave them a number of instances of other tribes in Liberia and parts of Africa that were being materially benefitted by such enterprises as he had outlined, and how the natives there were readily adapting themselves to new conditions.

"Instead of wars," he said, "and poverty and darkness, there is peaceful industry, progress, and prosperity. These blessings will be yours if you desire them."

He pointed out to them that it was only

through such means as the planting of religious and industrial missions that Africa will be reclaimed from the barbarity and superstition that has enveloped it for ages. He pleaded for their own sakes, the sake of their country, their children and wives, that they open their eyes to the importance of improving their condition by accepting the means which propose these ends.

"Do you wish this mission?" he concluded; "and if so, what will you do to help establish it? Lands, buildings, and protection need to be pledged before any step can be taken to its establishment. I represent no corporation backed by ample funds to set the work in operation, but am simply a private individual actuated by motives that crave your welfare. I am here on my own responsibility, making a study of the country, gathering reliable information with a view of furnishing the same to friends and organizations abroad, who are in search of open doors in Africa to spread the Gospel and civilization among heathen tribes."

Jarbar made sure of each word spoken by Mr. Jackson. There was difficulty in translating some of the speaker's sentences, due to the poverty of the native dialect, which lacks many ideas and expressions used by him, but this difficulty was obviated by the free use of parables, figures of speech, paraphrases and gestures in which native orators are adepts. From beginning to end he riveted attention, and the address met with that sanction from point to point that always accompanies African palavers, when the hearts of the natives are gratified.

But would the king and chiefs grant him the opportunity of fulfilling the desire of his heart?

CHAPTER V

The King Is Delighted By Project.— Chieftains Heartily Concur.— The King's Address.— He Confers With Liberian Government.

"Ha! Ha!" laughed the king, with a loud clap of his hands as he shifted in his hammock from the side on which he had lain during the course of the address, to the other.

He was pleased beyond expression by the hearty concurrence given the proposition by his twelve chieftains, who not only nodded assent throughout the speech, but shouted approval at its close and requested the singing girls to chant the praises of the "Merican" man whose words made their hearts "lay down." And then the air resounded with a medley of notes and noises from the singers and the town people who joined them.

The king turned to Ja Ja Nough, first in rank of his chieftains, and asked, "What say you?"

"That same thing you say, king, I say too," was the reply.

This query was passed in turn to each chief, and they followed the example of their senior in age and office, without alteration. Brief ceremonies followed, confirming their statements, by native oaths and a Gri-Gri Bush play, which occupied the balance of the evening.

On the next day at noon the king resumed the palaver and delivered his ultimatum in the Bassa-Gibi dialect.

"I and my chieftains have heard you," he said, "and we are thankful for your errand, Mr. Jackson. I might ask Commissioner Fisk to reply to you, but if I did so then you might infer from my silence that I was not able to make the response myself.

"If a man were searching for the bark of a tree to make a powerful medicine, and should swim across a wide and dangerous river for it, when the very tree he wanted was on the side of the river where he lived, he would not show good sense in imperiling his life needlessly.

"We are like the man searching for the powerful medicine. You have the medicine, and you have brought it within our reach. We are in need of the very thing you came to bring us—the powerful medicine of the white man—Book and "God palaver." You seem anxious to bring it to us. Would it show wisdom in us to turn you away? Why should we refuse a good thing when God sends it to our own country so plainly through one of His own messengers, who out of his own heart came so far to see us and enlighten our minds? If we say no, we do not want mission work, the opportunity may never come again, and we may then seek for it elsewhere, but in vain, for we foolishly ignored it when it came providentially to us.

"Let me ask you one thing. Does President Barclay know anything about your mission? If not, I must send him a book (letter) on the matter and secure his consent. But, as far as we are concerned, and as far as it is in our power to act, you have our hearty consent to come in our midst and establish a mission of whatever character and extent you and your supporters may desire. We have a country of large extent and very many people. We know much can be done here. Our people are strong, brave, and hospitable. We have never been whipped. We fought ten years, a long and bloody war, with the Pessy tribe. We now have peace. We need enlightenment. We invite you to come to us, and just as we have received and treated you since you have been in our midst, we will do the same by you as long as you remain with us. We have thousands of children in gross ignorance. We have long desired something better for them and for us.

"We need to know book (letters) and industries just like the Liberians on the beach. We will give you as much land as you wish,—one thousand acres, or more,—in the best location we can find in the whole country. You will have plenty of room for a big farm and all the industries you need. When you are well established you will not only be a help to us, but a protection also. We will appeal to you for help and advice when we need it. We will be one and will help each other. We will become better acquainted as we live side by side, you with us and we with you.

"Do you wish to see the place now, or do you wish to see it later? The only thing that we fear is that you may not return again after you leave us, to carry out what you have in mind. You have touched our hearts, and raised our expectations in telling us of the need and benefit of mission work in Gibi. Now, do not disappoint us. Tell your bishop and all your friends in Monrovia and America that we want you to come back to Gibi to be our father. May you come back again to us as you came first, and may the mission you tell us about become one that we can see with our eyes.

"(Signed) KIE TIPOOR,
"In behalf of his chieftains and people of Gibi.
His (x) mark.
"WILLIAM F. FISK,
"*African Commissioner Gibi Country.*
"J. RICHARDS, *Secretary.*"

The king conferred with Commissioner Fisk, official representative of the Liberian Government, whose court is at Kie Tipoor, on the subject, and a letter was transmitted to President Barclay, Chief Executive of the Republic.

The king, with his chieftains, exercises a large measure of local self-government, as a primary court, for all matters affecting his community and district. He has the co-operation of district commissioners as an appellate court. The commissioners are appointed by the President upon the recommendation of the Secretary of the Interior. Thus is ceded the traditional rights of native rulers, and is also recognized the supreme authority of the Executive Government.

The following is Commissioner Fisk's letter to President Barclay:

"Kie Tipoor, Gibi Country,
March 6, 1907.
"His Excellency, Arthur Barclay,
"*President of Liberia, Monrovia.*

"Sir—This comes to inform you that King Kie Tipoor, of the Gibi Country, is desirous of having mission work established in his country, and in response to Mr. John B. Jackson, of New York, who has been here for the past month studying the people and country and investigating the possibilities for mission work, if the opportunity for such work is offered him. The king, with the unanimous consent of his chieftains, has agreed, provided your consent and endorsement is given.

"I herewith enclose a copy of the king's reply to Mr. Jackson. The gentleman seems deeply impressed with the country and is anxious to promote the people's welfare. I would be happy to have him established here, where enlightenment is so much in demand, if he should find it possible to do so. The king and chiefs gave him every encouragement and heartily welcomed him. Knowing your own interest in the aboriginal population, and your statesmanlike efforts in their behalf, I am sure you will give executive countenance and support to an undertaking that promises so much for the development of the Hinterland and the advancement of the tribes inhabiting these regions.

"Hoping that the prospective work will meet with your approval, I am,

"Your obedient servant,
"W. H. Fisk,
"Chief Commissioner, Gibi Country, Liberia."

Jarbar's happiness equaled Mr. Jackson's as he saw the favorable impression the proposition made upon the entire court, especially when he interpreted the words of the king, and read the letter of the commissioner to the President. He recalled what Mr. Jackson had said on his arrival in the town: "Let us not despair; let us be patient and wait a little while. Perhaps conditions may be more favorable than we anticipate." Now matters had turned out most favorably, even beyond his expectations, and his joy was proportionately great.

He had lingered about the palaver house and had heard the familiar personal after-talks of the day's proceedings. This, together with the incidental remarks and gossip of the town, furnished a true index to the heart of the natives, and revealed their actual feeling on the subject. There were many hearty expressions of delight over all that was said. Estimates of Mr. Jackson and of what he proposed respecting the mission were most favorable, and the feeling was general that the project, if set on foot, would inaugurate a new era and bring immeasurable benefits to the tribes in those regions. This friendly attitude opened the way for closer relations. Confidence was inspired, and Mr. Jackson lost no time in extending his observations by easy talks in hut and grove, along the path, in forest and field wherever opportunity presented itself.

CHAPTER VI

TRIALS BY FIRE, SMOKE, AND SASSWOOD ANNOUNCED.—THE ACCUSATIONS.—THE YOUNG MEN INNOCENT.—THEY SEEK LAWFUL REVENGE.—THE TORTURE ONE YOUNG WOMAN IS PUT TO, AND HER FUTURE LIFE.

"THE Gri-Gri men at Tarplah's town have just announced that a number of persons are to undergo trials by fire, smoke, and sasswood to-day. The people from several of the neighboring towns have been summoned to meet there to witness the trial. It will be held in the center of the town within the view of everybody." Thus spoke Jarbar, in a voice revealing a feeling of profound regret.

"O, how dreadful!" exclaimed Mr. Jackson, distressfully.

"It is only one of the blind ways of the heathen. In their ignorance they resort to practices of the most revolting character. For centuries these things have been going on, and they will continue until their condition has been bettered by enlightenment."

"Have you learned the particulars of the several cases?"

"Well," answered Jarbar, "from what I have gathered, those who are to be tested by the fire ordeal are three men who live at Tarplah's town. They are his 'boys,' or servants. Tarplah, the head man of the town, traded off several of his goats and bullocks for a quantity of salt. The Pessey caravans that passed through here on their way to the Pessey country the other day carried several hundred bags of salt, along with other supplies, to the Dutch factory recently established farther inland. With them the barter was made.

"Now one of these bags of salt can not be found, although the whole town has been diligently searched for several days, and there is general uproar about the matter. Tarplah is furious. The 'boys,' tremblingly, have protested their innocence, but despite this they must be subjected to the torture prescribed by native law to establish their innocence or guilt."

"And, of course, this procedure is final, and the result unerring?" asked Mr. Jackson, with a feeling of disgust.

"Yes, quite so. But the second is the case of a woman, the head wife of a warrior who is now at the point of death. His illness is attributed to his wife, whom the "devil doctors" claim made witch for him with a powerful ju-ju. He is now under the spell of this mighty influence and will die. The fetich magicians, however, are making enchantments about his hut and in his room. They placed a potent ju-ju on his diseased body, but

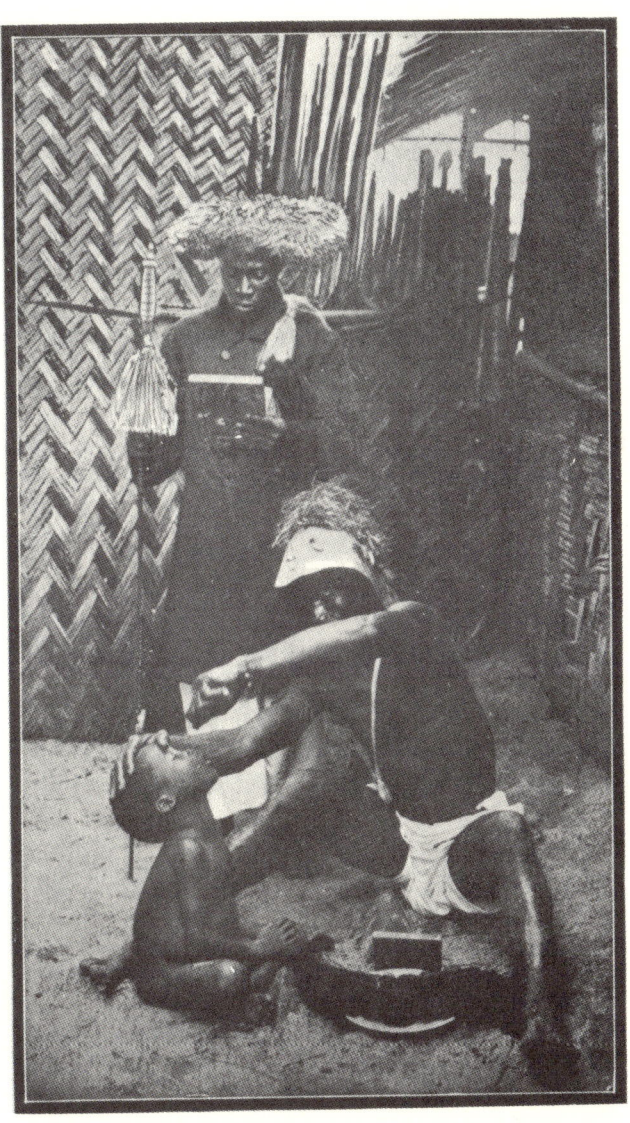

Witch Doctors Applying Local Remedies Combined with Occult Powers on Sick Child.

to no effect. The poor woman must be placed in smoke to force her to a confession of what she has never committed, and what she stoutly denies."

"Poor heathen woman! How deplorable her condition!" uttered Mr. Jackson, vehemently, and with a deep sigh he asked, "Who is the third?"

"Women again. Three women have unfortunately excited the spirit of jealousy in their distrustful and speculating lords, and to satisfy them must drink sasswood. They plead in tears and piteously prostrate themselves before their heartless masters, declaring their innocence and protesting their fidelity, but in vain."

"Gracious! Is there no relief?"

"There is none, while moral and spiritual night rests like a pall upon the people and continent. Rescue must come from without. Africa, in its superstition and degradation, can not save itself. With outstretched hands she pleads for help."

"And O, then, to the rescue! To the rescue!" fervently responded Mr. Jackson.

The tom-toms are in requisition; their dull, doleful strokes, like the tolling bell in civilization, stir feelings of gloom and sadness and betoken death. The people gather in crowds and gaze with morbid curiosity upon the trembling unfortunates, who, relying solely upon the potency of their gri-gri with its "charmed influence," face the trying ordeal with a certain indifference that is re-

MISSIONARY STORY SKETCHES

markable. For though like imprisoned birds their instinct is to escape from the awful wrongs and cruelties which heathenism throws about them, binding them as with iron chains, whither shall they flee? There is no escape except by moral emancipation. This is their only hope. It is this alone that enables mankind to cast off the chains and enter into life unmaimed and free.

The trial begins. The Gri-Gri men place a large pot filled with palm oil over a huge fire. It is soon hot and the oil begins to simmer and then to burn and blaze as the heat and flames increase in intensity. Small pieces of iron are placed in the bottom of the pot containing this boiling liquid fire, and the culprit is required to douse the bare hand and arm therein, taking out the deposits, which if done with impunity establishes his innocence beyond the shadow of a doubt.

But even to the untutored savage this is a severe ordeal, if not an absurd one, and to resist the action of the heat and mitigate the agony the hand and arm are smeared over with a viscid substance which forms a complete covering for the skin. This renders the flesh less susceptible to the heat. Thus the young men, being nerved to endurance by the consciousness of having committed no wrong and relying upon the virtue of their fetich, with muscles unmoved, one by one instantly plunge their arm in the boiling oil, removing the pieces of iron, and are thus declared innocent amid the wild shouts of the applauding crowd.

The wheel of fortune revolves in their favor, and it is now their turn to avenge the burning wrong committed against them. Native usage permits an infliction of punishment upon the accusers of a culprit declared innocent by the judges of the ordeal, and considerable latitude is given the acquitted. Emboldened by the shouts of approval and with the public sentiment supporting them, they seek vengeance and spite with all the bitterness and intensity of feeling which is possible to the injured pride of an irate and resentful savage.

Tarplah, to appease their wrath, is among the first to welcome them, and hastens to remove the stigma which the charge and ordeal has attached to the good names of the accused. Their character is vindicated, and the "boys" restored to the family of their master, again becoming members of his household.

But on the edge of the town, trembling with bowed heads, stand two other culprits who must next undergo the crucial test which heathenism requires. They are women—poor creatures! What sympathy and pity they excite as you look upon them! Their lips are moving nervously and a faint whisper discloses that they are innocent, but

MISSIONARY STORY SKETCHES

are willing, according to the custom of their country and tribe, to be subjected to any torture, however severe, feeling secure in the fetich, which composes their chief apparel and which they regard with idolatrous veneration and trust to guard and protect them from all harm.

The first woman is led by two men, with strong and ruthless hands, to the hut where her punishment is in waiting. She ascends the low roof of the thatch hut by means of a notched log which serves as a primitive ladder. On reaching the upper apartment, she is bound fast with native rope. Her face is turned downward, and on the hard earthen floor directly beneath is built, with one or two logs, a large fire.

As the flames increase, green branches are thrown on in piles, and to make the suffering as excruciating as possible, large handfuls of pepper are added. Great volumes of stifling, choking fumes of smoke issue from this, and the hut, already dark with smoke and stalactite forms of soot by ordinary uses of fire, is made even blacker by this act of cruelty.

The victim is thoroughly smoked, and the suffering becomes more intense as the test continues. But with Spartan-like composure this poor, defenseless creature endures the test, revealing physical weakness only where the body can not withstand the awful agony. The victim is

FOLK-LORE FROM AFRICA

seized with paroxysms of violent coughing and sneezing. The lungs and eyes, suffering the most, are highly inflamed, and receive serious injuries, which will last a lifetime.

The poor woman at last is taken down, more dead than alive. Stifled and dazed by the shock which the trial has given her, she is completely prostrated with exhaustion. She looks an object of despair, and mutely pleads for relief by her extreme helplessness and woe. Having stoutly declared her innocence of the crime of bewitching her husband, and having withstood the ordeal, she is free of the charge, but regarded as property.

She must be divided with the rest of the warrior's effects. She falls to a man whom she despises. Unwilling to receive him as her husband, she is bound hand and foot, and is ruthlessly dragged through the town and along the narrow, rugged path to the bank of the river, where a canoe bears her away to a distant town. After days of punishment and extreme suffering, she reluctantly yields to her sad fate, living a life of sorrow and drudgery to her unsympathetic lord.

Mr. Jackson witnessed this trial, and then muttered, "Enough; enough!" and calling Jarbar away from the crowd that followed the woman to the river, said, "Let us return to our quarters at Kie Tipoor."

"But there yet remains the trial by sasswood,"

protested Jarbar, "and that is now to follow. Will you not remain to witness it?"

"No, for my heart is sick of all these revolting scenes. How depressing they are! How they work upon the feelings, making the heart to bleed!"

"Yes," agreed Jarbar, "and the heathen themselves long for something better; they desire such a change of conditions as shall bring a speedy end to the long and terrible reign of darkness and degradation."

"I believe they do in their heart of hearts, notwithstanding their savage customs," said Mr. Jackson, and then he stood musing a while before taking up the return journey.

CHAPTER VII

"The Night is Far Spent; the Day is at Hand."

"I firmly believe," said Jarbar, halting with Mr. Jackson, and reciprocating his thoughtful mood, "that a better day is dawning for these inland tribes, so long unreached and deprived of the light."

Quoting from the words of the great Apostle to the Gentiles, in confirmation of his belief, he said, "The night is far spent; the day is at hand."

"How appropriate!" was the quick comment of Mr. Jackson. "I love those words, and believe in them thoroughly as specially applicable to Africa."

"Tell me," said Jarbar, "what your interpretation of those words is, and what application you would make of them in reference to this particular field."

"Well, in the first place, they have a large scope and meaning. To fully understand them we must know the chain of thoughts which precedes.

"The apostle Paul opens the chapter with an interesting discussion on the duty of Christians to the State in the light of the Lord's second coming, and in the power of His presence. As a spiritual guide and teacher of the Church, the apostle would have Christians thoroughly established in the political principles of the new faith, and the mysterious society of which they were recent communicants.

"He aims to show them their true relation to the State as individual Christians, or a group of Christians. His point is to have them supremely loyal to the powers that be, thoroughly imbued with the spirit of obedience and submission, and fortified by patriotic principles. This was the surer and speedier way to the victory which they earnestly craved—the victory which was at last to overcome the world.

"The Pauline conception of civic duty, therefore, was that the attitude of Christians to the State must not be that of revolutionists or socialists, looking upon the State or Government as a sort of belligerent power, against which they were to direct assaults or wage incessant warfare, but they were to be law-abiding and patriotic. Even though the law might be severe and the ruler despotic, Christians should still remember that civil government in principle is of God, and must be supported. Law and order must be maintained. In this rested the safety, perpetuity, and prosperity of the State and Church also. 'Fear God, honor the king,' should ever be their motto.

FOLK-LORE FROM AFRICA

"This seemed timely and judicious admonition, for Nero, the tyrant, would soon bear rule, and Christians would pay dearly for their allegiance to the lowly Nazarene. Shortly this cruel despot would immortalize his reign by burning them in the imperial gardens as lamps, and a cruel Trojan, regarding Christianity as a 'contagious superstition,' and Christian steadfastness and heroism as 'inflexible obstinacy,' would officially decree their death.

"The Christians, as exponents of the new faith, needed such instruction as he gives here to establish them in right principles and mark out their course and line of action. Much would be expected of them, and they were to demonstrate the inward virtue of Christianity. Their greatest triumphs were to come by patient, loyal suffering, and enduring hardships as good soldiers. They were ever to be witnesses for right and truth, even before tyrants and heartless persecutors remaining firm and loyal to God and State.

"And closing the chapter, the apostle considers the condition of the whole Gentile world under the similitude of night, with its deepening shadows and gloom, and the sinful practices which darkness facilitates. But this is only transient; its end is rapidly approaching, to be followed by the dawning day, soon to be radiant and glorious.

"This new period is the Gospel era, and the

MISSIONARY STORY SKETCHES

Gentile world, once shrouded in moral and spiritual night, is to welcome the Sun of Righteousness with healing in His wings. To them are to come the full benefits of the atonement through Jesus Christ, the Light of Salvation.

"He sounds a clarion note of alarm for Christians to awake from sleep, the sleep of indifference, shaking off their spiritual lethargy and robing themselves with the habiliments of light.

"Africa, like the Roman world in St. Paul's day, is heathen. The general condition of her people is that of moral night; but that night of heathenism is growing old, in view of the full-orbed day of this twentieth century civilization.

"The duty of Christians as individuals and as organizations is plain and urgent. They owe a debt to the heathen world which they are in duty bound to pay, or else their integrity as Christians must be seriously impaired and their loyalty prove merely an empty pretension. That Africa's millions should still grope in darkness is a reproach to the zeal of Christians and a challenge to the Church of Christ. Liberia's unreached millions have claims that should no longer be ignored. They demand immediate and adequate consideration."

"I am very grateful to you for the presentation you have given of this passage of Scripture. I thoroughly indorse your views. What a tremen-

FOLK-LORE FROM AFRICA

dous responsibility, indeed, rests upon Christendom to give the Gospel and its attendant blessings to the Christless millions of earth, and specially benighted Africa." Jarbar spoke with a tremor in his voice, and in his eyes the tears gathered, for the earnest words of Mr. Jackson went straight to his heart.

"Thank you, dear brother. I have always felt that duty deeply myself, but now it seems more imperative since I have seen so much with my own eyes and heard so much with my own ears. While looking upon these scenes of cruelty and darkness, and thinking of the moral debt we owe to Africa, I recall the lines of a stirring hymn I once heard sung in England at a Wesleyan Methodist Conference:

> " The heathen perish day by day,
> Thousand on thousand pass away!
> O Christians, to their rescue fly,
> Preach Jesus to them ere they die.
>
> Wealth, labor, talents, freely give,
> Yea, life itself, that they may live;
> What hath your Savior done for you,
> And what for Him will ye not do?
>
> Thou Spirit of the Lord, go forth,
> Call in the south, wake up the north;
> In every clime, from sun to sun,
> Gather God's children into one.''

MISSIONARY STORY SKETCHES

"Beautiful sentiments! Glorious era portrayed for the Kingdom! May that prayer be fully answered, and may the long-promised day of salvation speedily come for Africa!" said Jarbar.

"Allow me also to add," said Mr. Jackson, "that the day will come when the heathen shall be given as an inheritance and the uttermost parts of the earth as a possession, when 'Thy way may be known upon the earth, Thy saving health among all nations;' when 'All thy children shall be taught of the Lord;' when 'Out of Zion shall go forth law' and . . . 'When princes shall come out of Egypt; Ethiopia shall stretch out her hands unto God;' . . . when 'The wilderness and the solitary place shall be glad for them; and the desert shall rejoice and blossom as the rose;' when 'The parched ground shall become a pool, and the thirsty land springs of water; in the habitation of dragons, where each lay, shall be grass with reeds and rushes. And an highway shall be there, and a way, and it shall be called the way of holiness; the unclean shall not pass over it; but it shall be for those; the wayfaring man, though fools, shall not err therein. And the ransomed of the Lord shall return, and come to Zion with songs, and everlasting joy upon their heads; they shall obtain joy and gladness, and sorrow and sighing shall flee away.' Then 'they shall sit every man under his vine, and his fig tree, and none shall make them afraid.'"

"Come that day will for Africa; but, O Lord, may it come in our day, speedily, speedily!" was the solemnly, hopeful refrain of hearts, which, though twain, yet beat as one, in perfect harmony and accord.

CHAPTER VIII

A Walk In a Beautiful Forest, "Where Nature Speaks Ever with God."—"Rum Ketch Dem Place Far Pass Kie Tipoor."—A Covenant Sealed.—A Night's Conversation With a King In Liberia's Wilderness, and What Characteristics it Revealed.

The two men had left Tarplah's town, the scene of the trial by fire, smoke, and sasswood, and were on their way to their temporary abode at Kie Tipoor. The town was soon lost to view by the many hills and groves in their course as they journeyed on. Soon, also, the barbaric shouts and noises of the people died away, and they were left alone in the heart of the forest, to the sweeter and more ennobling music of nature's realm.

Their routes lay through a tedious but magnificent stretch of woods, which they entered after many a bend and turn of the rough and crooked path. The sun was just rising. Its emerald light made by penetration through the deep, rich green foliage of the forest, and shining upon the broad, green leaves of the trees and shrubbery which held the dew and rain of the previous night, bathed the whole woodland with a mellow refreshment.

FOLK-LORE FROM AFRICA

In the giant tree-tops, whose wide-spreading branches formed a vast natural canopy overhead, were heard enchanting love-notes of a chorus of birds, merrily chirping to their mates. Springing from limb to limb, in gleeful, mischievous spirit, performing a thousand pranks, were hordes of monkeys, conspicuous among which were the Bay-thighed Diana family, charming creatures, reveling in their unrivaled beauty of color and figure. Numerous rivulets, flowing over beds of sand and gravel, joining other streams, emptied themselves into rivers on whose calm surface floated fragrant lilies and blended images of sky and shore. On their banks grew in gorgeous profusion wild flowers and palms; festoons of parasitic plants hung from the tops of the tallest trees to the water's edge.

Amid these forest scenes our friends conversed in loving fellowship on themes of far-reaching import, each burning with desire that the way might be opened that their conception of duty with respect to their brethren in the Liberian wilderness might speedily assume tangible and practical form.

"Yonder is Kie Tipoor! Pleasing aspect!" each thought as they stood together upon the top of a high hill overlooking the surrounding country and gazed intently toward the east, where the town lay where the king of the Gibi people resides. At the base of the hill was Budoo's town, with its cluster of houses, and three miles away were half towns. Between lay the open clearings where the natives grow their meager farms of rice, cassava, edoes, potatoes, and coffee. Their cattle were lazily grazing in the meadows near by.

A branch of the Farmington or Junk River wended its way a quarter of a mile from the hill. This is the water supply of the town, as well as a highway for native traffic. A huge tree uprooted by a terrific tornado lay across the river from bank to bank, forming a perfect and convenient bridge for pedestrians. The banks of the river, which form quite a bluff here, lifted the huge tree at considerable elevation. To facilitate crossing, the natives had flattened the top and cut many notches in it to prevent slipping in the rainy season.

The river dashes down from the heart of Liberia, and makes its way circuitously to the ocean. Its waters here are transparent and have the purity and excellence which only the health-giving mountain and forest region can impart. The town is embosomed in a cluster of fruit-bearing trees, composed of bread-fruit, bananas, plantains, oranges, and limes, the appearance of which was attractive as they looked down upon them from the hill.

"How long do you think it will take us to reach the town?" asked Mr. Jackson.

"O, not long; an hour of steady walking will put us there," answered Jarbar.

FOLK-LORE FROM AFRICA

They entered the plains, with their tall grasses; and such was the rankness and density of the grass and bush, they were completely hidden amidst the mass and confusion of jungle. The path was beset by luxuriant weeds, and it was not possible to see on what they were walking. The heavy dew gave them a thorough drenching, and they found it necessary to stop frequently to ring the water from their clothing.

But soon the grassy plain was behind them and they reached an open country. Stopping at a straggling town, they removed their wet clothing, and, after climbing a few more hills and crossing several streams, reached their quarters just as the sun was setting.

The weariness of bush-traveling was telling on the physical condition of Mr. Jackson, who showed it in his face and labored movements. But a night or two of absolute rest would recuperate his energies and render him equal to the task before him.

The king's head wife was busy preparing supper for His Majesty's stranger, now quite a familiar figure about the town and district. The meal was characteristic—*dumboy* and pepper soup with venison. The soup was flavored with palm oil and highly seasoned with pepper. While eaten not without difficulty, yet Mr. Jackson's sojourn among these simple folk of nature had made him remarkably less fastidious about many things, chief

MISSIONARY STORY SKETCHES

of which was his food. He had learned to obey implicitly the apostolic injunction of eating whatsoever was set before him, asking no questions for conscience' sake.

To do otherwise among savage peoples was simply to starve. His appetite was voracious, and he suffered no ill-effects from what he ate, although taken from the extensive and undiscriminating range of heathen dietary. On general principles he ate everything dished up for food, trusting to the judgment of the natives, which seemed admirably sound in many other things. He was astonished to learn what a variety of strange and uninviting foods one might eat when without the pale of civilization, and yet survive. In one thing, however, he reserved the right to draw the line, and that was in feasting on human flesh. But that, to his knowledge, was never served.

After eating a hearty supper in the "country kitchen," Mr. Jackson came into the house for a social chat before retiring for the night, and swung to and fro in the native hammock, which was suspended diagonally across the room. The hammock belonged to the king, and in it he was accustomed to take his daily siesta.

The quarters given him were the most spacious in the town, and the room in which the hammock was stretched was unusually large. It was filled with natives, who squatted together around him

FOLK-LORE FROM AFRICA

on the hard mud floor. Among them was the king, who occupied a wooden stool in the center of the group. In the middle of the floor was the fireplace, containing a heap of ashes. The smoldering ends of two logs, placed together, emitted a fickle flame, which furnished the occasional and only light in the dark room. A steady curl of smoke streaming from the embers made it difficult for all but the natives to remain in the little hut. The window in the sleeping apartment adjoining was the only escape for the nuisance.

Motioning to Jarbar to interpret for him, one of the company, removing an old foul pipe from his mouth, after vigorously sucking it and puffing from it fumes of offensive smoke, passed it to another. The pipe had thus gone the entire rounds, the women and children, even those in their mother's arms, sharing in the doubtful luxury. He uttered something in his native tongue that had an outlandish ring. All of the crowd except the king united in saying the same thing. It was followed by uproarious laughter.

"What are they saying?" queried Mr. Jackson, with some eagerness.

"I am sorry to tell you," answered the interpreter.

The men had again spoken in a chorus of voices, as before, but in a more emphatic way.

"They say," said Jarbar, "that their throats

are dry and have not been wet since the stranger's sojourn in their midst. In other words, they ask you for rum."

"Rum?"

"Yes; that is what their request means," nodded Jarbar.

"How sad!" pathetically exclaimed Mr. Jackson.

They suspected, from the careful study of the stranger that they had made, that their petition would be met with a prompt rebuff; but they ventured to ask. They had watched his luggage, and were curious to know what he had concealed in some packages that had not been opened. Some of the group fancied that perhaps these contained the liquid fire their appetites craved.

"Tarlow!"

"Heh?"

"Come here!"

Tarlow immediately dragged himself nearer to Mr. Jackson. His movement created a little commotion among the crowd. He had lived in the Liberian settlements, on the coast, and could speak a little broken English. He had been down the West African coast as a laborer on board the German, Spanish, and English steamers, calling at Liberian ports, and had seen much of the evil effects of New England rum and Holland gin upon the natives. He was a resident in the town, and

FOLK-LORE FROM AFRICA

Mr. Jackson wanted to speak to him and through him to the people.

"Tell me, Tarlow," said he, "is rum brought out this far in the interior?"

Tarlow laughed outright. And when he had "passed" (interpreted) the question to the crowd, they yelled lustily; all in good humor, however. Speaking excitedly, and accompanying his words with a gesture, pointing toward the Pessey country, he said: "Rum ketch dem place far pass Kie Tipoor! In dem kingjar, rum lib dah plenty. Pessey people toat um for he country."

This testimony, thought the natives, was convincing argument for compliance with their request, should their surmises be well founded.

Tarlow continued: "Dem first stranger dat come we country for trade he bring too much rum. Dem rum he waste for ground (thrown upon the ground). Bassa men no like him den. He no saby (understand) um. Now he like um plenty. He be fine. He—"

"But rum, Tarlow," interrupted Mr. Jackson, "is bad; it makes people foolish; it hurts them. It kills them, and—"

Tarlow stared wildly, and his broad grin revealed his white teeth. The crowd, catching the contagion of his emotions, drowned the voice of Mr. Jackson by their commotion.

But Mr. Jackson continued: "Thousands of

natives suffer from its baneful effects and find from it an early grave."

To this the gray-haired king nodded assent, and groaned deeply as it was interpreted. This signal was decisive in turning the tide on the side of Mr. Jackson. Out of respect for the king, defense for rum and further request for it would have been impolite. So the champions for demon Alcohol were put to silence.

But a leader of this element, addressing Tarlow, said: "Tarlow, dem daddy say rum be bad—he kill we people; he do all dem bad ting. He mouth no lie bit, but he no tell we who make dem rum. We no make um. He come from big, big 'Merica and Europe. Steamer bring um we country. White man make um. White man saby book; black man no saby book. S'pose rum be bad; what for white man make um? To kill we? S'pose white man stop for make um; stop for send um we country; we no drink him den. We no die."

Wooseh, the speaker, sat down amid tremendous applause, and he was not indifferent to their compliment. The party whose views he expressed, as well as the rest, felt that he had scored a victory.

"Good!" shouted Mr. Jackson; "but more important it is to begin now with ourselves to create sentiment against the evil, and break up our appetite for it. It is, after all, not what others do, but what we do ourselves, that matters. Let *us* get straight. If we stop using it, the ships will stop bringing it to us.

"Aha! Aha!" exclaimed the king, immensely pleased. "True, true! I agree. I have stopped years ago, and purpose never more to touch it. It nearly ruined me several years ago. I would keep it entirely out of my country if I could."

The Gri-Gri men suggested that all bind themselves according to their custom, with an oath on their fetich, against the evil. It was made and "eaten," and under the glare of a bamboo torch, which was made specially for the purpose, the covenant was sealed. As Mr. Jackson looked upon their crude ceremony under the light of the torch, he was much impressed with the earnestness that actuated them. In his heart he wished that a similar step would be taken among all the natives where the curse of drink has entered with its awful blight.

It is no exaggeration to say that there exists no greater enemy to Africa and her peoples than this debasing evil. It is a great obstacle to the progress of civilization there, and is spreading desolation and ruin, far worse than superstition and barbarism. Thousands of poor, deluded natives are daily sinking to still lower depths of sin and shame by this poison that unprincipled merchants are constantly importing in increasing quantities, destroying stalwart humanity, soul and body.

MISSIONARY STORY SKETCHES

The following note, which appeared in an English paper interested in West Africa, reveals how the ruin of a helpless continent is persistently effected, without remorse or compunction of conscience on the part of those who commit this unpardonable sin against God and mankind:

"The civilization of Africa goes apace. A Hamburg correspondent writes me that a British steamer sailed thence the other day with one thousand tons weight of spirits on board for Lagos and Southern Nigeria. He also says that another steamer is due to leave in a few days for the same destination, with nearly double that amount on board. The spirits, he writes, consist of bad gin and worse rum, and the trade is principally in the hands of a few big English and German firms."

There is but one right attitude toward this evil. It is perpetual and uncompromising opposition.

"The people are coming from Tarplah's town," said Wooseh, excitedly.

This was the scene of the trial by fire, smoke, and sasswood, a few days before. As they approached Kie Tipoor the uproar they made was deafening.

Mr. Jackson seized this opportunity to bring up the subject of sasswood, since the discussion of rum had had such a satisfactory conclusion.

FOLK-LORE FROM AFRICA

"What is sasswood?" he inquired.

Jarbar interpreted for King Kie Tipoor, who volunteered to answer all the questions on the subject. "It is a small piece of bark ground to powder and dissolved in water," he said, "and the sasswood tree is sacred."

"It is sacred, you say?"

"Yes," and with a gesture to convey an idea difficult to express in words, said, "the powers of divination inhere in its bark."

"How is it administered?"

"A person accused of witch, theft, or any other crime worthy of this test, is made to drink this poisonous draft. Four heavy doses at intervals are given."

"What has that to do with either confirming or acquitting the culprit?" asked Mr. Jackson.

"Everything," said the king. "According to our belief, if the sasswood is disgorged the subject is innocent of the charge and is spared; if it kills, he is guilty."

"Then you must have many deaths resulting from sasswood," said Mr. Jackson.

"Yes; but not as many now as in former years."

"What has made the number diminish?"

"Civilized law is against it now."

"Are you not glad, king, of that?"

"Yes, very."

MISSIONARY STORY SKETCHES

"What becomes of the personal effects of the condemned culprit; his relatives, also?"

"Property is confiscated or destroyed; relatives are dishonored."

"Is recourse to sasswood as a punishment always with good intentions?"

"No," replied the king, decidedly. "Oftentimes it is intended to serve only as a means for spite, to vent the spleen of infuriated chiefs, and to frighten the people into subjection. I am glad a better day is coming for my people, and in my heart I welcome all these improvements. But I want more of them, and less of civilized vices. I am thoroughly tired of heathenism."

"May all of your wants be granted, king!" said Mr. Jackson, fervently.

"But what became of the three women?" asked Mr. Jackson, inquisitively.

"Sasswood no ketch him," came from a trio of gruff voices. The men were peering in at the door. "Dem women he lib! He no die!" they said, exultantly.

"Then," said Mr. Jackson, "let us cheer for their providential deliverance!"

His suggestion was immediately carried out, and the varied voices, ranging in tone from the lowest bass to the highest notes reached by female voices, demonstrated the capacity, volume, and strength of African lungs and throats and revealed the tender feeling there lies hidden beneath the rough exterior of the heathen for those of their kith and kin.

By this time the night was advancing, and weariness settled upon the greater part of the motley group, who found it difficult to retain their interest in the evening's proceedings.

The crowd dispersed. They filed out one by one, as the little door would admit of no other method of exit. King Kie Tipoor lingered behind, as though anxious to speak. Coming nearer to Mr. Jackson, he said, "I want to talk a little with you alone." His tall and athletic figure looked kingly and noble in its primitive strength and maturity. Earnestness was in his accents and mien.

"Sit down, king," said Mr. Jackson. "There is always time to talk with you."

He drew his low stool nearer. The two men, guest and king, teacher and scholar, Christian and pagan, the latter ruler of a vast heathen district, sat until the small hours of the night, familiarly talking on those things which have interested mankind, civilized and heathen, ever since the world began.

Suffice it to say that the teacher found far out in Liberia's wilderness an apt and clever pupil, in

MISSIONARY STORY SKETCHES

whose breast was a genuine and insatiate longing to have brought to his country peaceful arts of industry and the blessings of salvation.

Should Christian America do less for Africa than give to this king and his people that which they crave and cryingly need?

CHAPTER IX

MR. JACKSON SPENDS A DAY VISITING THE TOWNS AND HALF TOWNS WITH THE KING.—HE MAKES OBSERVATIONS.—WHAT HE JOTTED DOWN AT THE CLOSE OF THE DAY BY THE LIGHT OF A TORCH.

EVEN before the sun had risen, the next morning the natives were up and going to their farms. Mr. Jackson had only one more day, according to his program, to remain at Kie Tipoor before taking his leave of the hospitable king and people for the coast, where he would pay his respects to the president and then immediately embark on a German steamer for the United States, by way of England.

He had made an engagement for the following day with the king, with whom he was to hold an interview on various topics and visit the farms and huts of his subjects.

"The king is sending now his messenger, I believe," said Jarbar, as he looked out of the windows that opened toward the king's quarters. A man came directly to the hut and asked to see Mr. Jackson.

"What is your errand?" he was asked.

MISSIONARY STORY SKETCHES

"King Kie Tipoor sent me for call dem daddy," said the boy. "He lib for go farm one time."

"Tell him I shall come immediately," said Mr. Jackson, and immediately the man was off with the message to the king.

On arriving at the king's house he found His Majesty had donned his working garb, which consisted only of a pair of mandingo trousers, loosely fitting about the loins, the legs of which reached down to the knees. The royal breast and arms lay bare. Sandals made of bark and fastened to the feet by means of tough grass were a protection against pebbles and roots. A cap made of African grass and dyed of leaves rested jauntily on the head.

His "boys" carried the farm implements, which consisted of short hoes, cutlasses, bill hooks, and small axes. His wives, three hundred in number, performed the farm work. Those at his headquarters were all in line, to the farm. The others were scattered about at his other towns and half towns within a radius of ten or twelve miles. The women looked like pack-horses, loaded down with burdens. On their backs they carried their infants, while pots for cooking the food on the farm were nicely balanced on their heads as they walked along. Both hands were holding implements used in farm work.

FOLK-LORE FROM AFRICA

The king worked a few hours himself, as it was the time known among the natives as "farm cutting" time, when their farms are cleared of brush and burned, preparatory to planting seed.

Leaving the farm, the day was spent in visiting a number of places where the natives were at work, Mr. Jackson busily making observations, which he jotted down at night, under the flickering light furnished by a bamboo torch and palm-oil lamp, as follows:

Women perform much of the heavy work, such as bringing wood and water, and cultivating the farms. It is not an unusual thing to see men lolling in hammocks while the women labor for food. Women do not eat with the men, but with the children or some other female friend. They are kept busy with farm life, basket, mat and fish-net making; drying seeds, fish, and meat for food, and picking and preparing cotton for the men to weave into cloth.

Many of the natives are skillful at weaving mats, making baskets, caps, fish-traps of bamboo, grass, and palm leaf. They also make ornaments of gold, silver, iron, and leather to decorate their bodies. Some of the country cloths made of cotton and the threads dyed with the juices of vegetable substances are very pretty and neatly made. Useful vessels are made from clay, such as pots, water jars, basins, and pipes. These are decorated with geometrical figures. Some work is done in wood carving also. Mortars for cleaning coffee

MISSIONARY STORY SKETCHES

and rice are made from logs, also canoes used for traveling upon the rivers and streams. The loom on which the native cloth is made is an important article in every household where this fabric is woven. Spoons, bowls, combs, and wooden images are also to be seen in nearly every town. They also make many useful articles of iron on their forges. Iron ore is abundant, and is found in most sections of the country. Some of these articles are the hoe, hatchet, knives, swords, needles, arrowheads, daggers, and rings for ornaments worn upon the arms and ankles.

The natives are fond of dancing and music. On moonlight nights they enjoy this into the late hours of the night. It is a common saying that when the moon is full all of Africa dances, and all night. The horn and drum are favorite musical instruments. To the ear of the stranger it is more noise than music, but by the native nothing better is desired. They also have many other native instruments. Sometimes imported music boxes or an accordion, or flutina, is used.

Among the Mandingoes there is a piano. It is about three feet long and has fifteen pieces of wood mounted over small bellow goads, and is played by two small sticks with rubber attached upon the end. Strips of leather are fastened to the hands, iron is attached to this, and to the iron, rings.

The African is light-hearted and sociable, and in this relation he enjoys himself immensely. Women dance with women, and men with men. Their dancing is not very graceful, as it consists

FOLK-LORE FROM AFRICA

of a slow movement to the center of the ring, which they form, and a rapid retreat. Each one takes a turn at this performance, while the others stand by clapping their hands and yelling loudly, making a perfect babel, of which the stranger soon tires. The regularity with which the body is moved to the music of the drum or horn is remarkable. A sort of clown usually accompanies the dance.

Smoking and using snuff is much indulged in by the natives of both sexes, both old and young. The natives seem to love to smoke, but it is very seldom that they are seen chewing tobacco.

African children are usually covered with charms and fetiches, to guard them against general or partial evil. Children are generally very healthy. Out-of-door life and simplicity in living do much for them in this respect.

Religiously, the African is the child of some "charmed influence." To him the universe is controlled by spirit, and his creed is to be in perfect harmony with the world of spirits. He is ever alert to protect himself against the forces of evil about him. His faith rests in the fetich. Through its potency life may be prolonged, death vanquished, and miracles performed. Many mysterious demonstrations are performed by diviners, or sandmen, who are adepts in occult mysteries. They are dexterous in the making of characters in the sand, from which symbols they divine events. In this art the outside world knows but little what Africans claim to do.

MISSIONARY STORY SKETCHES

In the Gibi country the Bassas worship a huge rock, and mountain also; the spirits of their fathers dwelling in the cave. The tribe is very superstitious.

Polygamy is practiced in almost every heathen town in Liberia. It is not diminishing. Among the Bassas there is no limit to the number of wives a man may have if he can purchase them. The question of polygamy is stubborn and colossal. The Christian Church in Liberia has a giant antagonist in this deeply-rooted and universal system among the heathen.

African children are just like children the world over. They love to play and to imitate their elders. The law of child-life in Africa is play; they enjoy themselves at foot races, wrestling, building tiny mud houses, tossing stones in the air, carrying bundles on their heads as they see their elders, molding clay into pots, bowls, basins, and pipes, digging in the ground with sticks. They become expert at making the bow and arrow. The woods resound with the noisy melody of their songs. They will pound in the mortar as though beating coffee or rice, and become skillful in handling the fanner for removing the chaff from coffee or rice.

The general health of the native in the interior is excellent. Sickness is not common; usually where it exists it may be traced from contagious diseases brought from the coast. The comparative absence of flies and mosquitoes make malaria scarce, if

Young Aspirants for Athletic Honors.

FOLK-LORE FROM AFRICA

not entirely absent. The various diseases prevalent on the coast among the civilized natives do not exist in the healthful uplands of the back country. The atmosphere is dry and pure. Tuberculosis is not known there. The out-of-door simple life of the natives, the pure air of the forest, their diet, which is principally vegetable, and their dwellings and scant apparel so wisely adapted to tropical conditions, contribute to health, strength of body, and longevity.

A sick-bush is a native hospital, located in the forest. When the king is critically ill he is taken there. Its location is a secret. Only one path leads to it, and only a confidential few know of it, such as the head warrior, some leading woman in the community or district. It is placed in charge of a nurse, who ministers to the sick king. The king's illness is communicated to no one. No bulletins announce the news of his condition. Should he die, the fact is not disclosed for some time, especially if the country is threatened by war. The reason is obvious. The king is head of the district or tribe, and if death is announced before a strong man sufficiently impresses himself upon the people, to succeed the king, the interests of the tribe may suffer.

Every town contains a palaver house. There is a large pole in the center, thirty or forty feet long. It has a conically-shaped roof and is covered with thatch. The floor is of hard-beaten clay and is higher than the surrounding surface. An embankment probably a foot and a half or two feet high is sometimes around the outer border, and this gives seats for the many visitors to this busy center of the native town.

These houses are used for the transaction of all the civil duties of the townsfolk, for the reception of strangers, and for such functions as may from time to time be held.

Another important house in each town is known as the house for strangers. These are usually large and airy and comfortable, and are used by the many strangers passing through the towns from time to time.

A system of barter obtains in the interior. Coin and paper money as used in the coast settlements are not used. Tobacco, rum, gin, salt, and other merchandise constitute money. In some sections of the interior women are the traders. They handle everything except native cloth. That is reserved for men.

Cotton grows abundantly in some sections of interior Liberia, and weaving is carried on to a great extent among some tribes, especially the Mandingoes. The sugar-cane flourishes too, and plantains and bananas grow in endless profusion.

The soil is fertile, and a large range of edible and commercial products may be cultivated. But the natives do not know the full value of agriculture. Their farm life is meager and rather fitful; amid great riches of soil and luxuriant vegetable growth, they are poor, because ignorant of the possibilities within their reach. Certain seasons of the year, known as "hungry times," are more or less frequent, because of the fickleness with which the soil is cultivated. And yet there is no end to the vast amount of natural productions and wealth that may be had from the earth, if the natives could be taught better agricultural methods and systematic tilling.

The drawbacks to farm life are many. While the soil is loose and fertile, yet vegetable life is rank and stubborn. Farm implements are inadequate; there are no plows to turn up the fallow ground. A short, crooked hoe is used, with which the ground is simply scratched. This hoe is not more than four inches wide; its handle is about twelve inches in length. Farm clearings are about one acre in extent; this is attended only a short while, and other clearings are made.

The forest is cleared by cutting down the trees with a small ax or hatchet. In preparing for farms, the rank brush, vines, and trees are cut down, and after they are dry they are burned. This process is known as "cutting farm."

Superstitions are carried into farm life. A death in a town is sufficient cause for leaving the place and opening up a farm elsewhere. There are farm fetiches to make the farm yield abundantly and to offset curses upon it by unfriendly and envious neighbors.

Sword-grass covers the path in many places in the interior, and makes travel difficult. It cuts the flesh and causes a wound that is difficult to heal.

MISSIONARY STORY SKETCHES

In some sections salt is transported in what is known as "salt sticks." They are strips of bamboo about three feet long and three inches in diameter. These are closely packed with salt, and the ends covered with leaves. The salt can not get wet when carried in this way. One person usually carries from fifteen to twenty of these sticks for a load. Fifty sticks of salt will buy a bullock.

Salt is also a sign of peace, and is used in settling difficulties between tribes. It is an article much in demand, and almost everything can be purchased with it.

Plantain leaves are often burned to obtain the alkali, which is a substitute for salt.

It is thought by those who do not know the African that there is not much affection among them. This is not correct, as the close observer will find that there is a tender relation existing, especially between mother and children. We witnessed scenes that were pathetic and touching when parents had been separated from their children and were united again. Mothers take their children in their arms and lavish upon them the same affection that a civilized mother would.

Natives have no accurate way of computing time. They measure it usually by the moon; hence, in starting on a journey, they state the time they expect to reach their destination in "moons." They work a certain number of moons for a certain amount of pay. In answer to a question as to how old they are, they will reply, "I was born in the rainy season, and am so many 'rains' old," or so

FOLK-LORE FROM AFRICA

many "dries" old. The age of a child may be approximately ascertained by the number of rice farms that have been planted since its birth.

Distances are measured by days' walk.

It is surprising with what facility and speed news is communicated from village to village and district to district, stretching into vast distances among the natives, notwithstanding the many obstacles attending forest traveling in the interior. Messages are quickly dispatched on pressing and important business, and ere the uninitiated is aware of the fact, miles of forest and jungle have been traversed by the tough and nimble feet of the native courier, who considers one or two hundred miles of wilderness travel as a rather easy jaunt.

Messages are conveyed by means of firing guns, tapping of drums and tom-toms under a well-wrought-out system or code of rappings which the native operator deftly executes. Their signals are usually made during the quiet hours of the night, when sound travels easily.

Poisoned arrows are used in warfare by the natives. The poison is made from a mixture of vegetable substances and is fatal in its effects. The least abrasion is death-dealing.

Open courts roofed with thatch, closely resembling a pavilion, are built in every town for the use of travelers.

Native houses for private uses are mostly built of mud and roofed with thatch. Mud is first

MISSIONARY STORY SKETCHES

banked two or three feet above the ground to insure dryness, also as a check to various insects and reptiles. This mud is beaten hard and is not unlike a cement floor when dry. Sometimes the walls are plastered over with clay or made of sun-dried bricks. There are few windows, except on the coast, where the houses are more on the style of the dwellings of civilized lands. There are usually two rooms, a sort of kitchen and the sleeping quarters. Fire is made in the center of the mud floor by placing the ends of logs together, and there the cooking is done.

The furniture of the native hut is very simple and not extensive. In some houses you will find small bamboo stools, mud or bamboo beds, hammocks, mats, water jars, drinking cups, cooking pots, and perhaps a few blocks of wood used as seats and pillows. Interior natives are adopting the use of imported articles rapidly, such as brass kettles, plates, bowls, spoons, knives, and forks. Natives along the coast have many pieces of furniture such as would be found in the houses of the civilized: bedsteads, chairs, tables, clocks, dishes, etc.

CHAPTER X

"Where are Our Carriers?" — "They Must be Rescued!" — Man and Beast in Deadly Combat. — A Strange Occurrence. — "Safe! Safe!"

Completing the task of note-making, Mr. Jackson turned to the one of gathering his things together for his departure.

Suddenly a disturbing thought made him pause and ask rather nervously: "Jarbar, what has become of our carriers? Come to think of it, I have not seen them for several days."

"Nor have I," was the reply.

"But they must be found, for we leave at daybreak."

"I wonder if those fellows have foolishly wandered off in the forest and have become lost," surmised Jarbar, quickly; but before waiting for a reply he rushed out of the door and hurriedly gathered several natives around him, whom he questioned eagerly concerning the whereabouts of the "boys."

Mr. Jackson was not a little alarmed. He had been absorbed in his interviews with the king, and his study of the people and country, and these

MISSIONARY STORY SKETCHES

things for the time being had occupied all his thoughts. But he hoped that Jarbar would succeed in locating them with the aid of the natives, who knew every nook and corner of the forest, so he addressed himself energetically to his packing.

Meanwhile Jarbar was questioning excitedly Somah and Zindeh, "Have you seen our boys anywhere?"

Somah, having a small stock of English at his command, said, "Yes;" Zindeh nodded assent and spoke affirmatively in his native tongue.

"Where? Pray tell me immediately!" cried Jarbar.

"In the big bush, one day's walk from here," said Somah.

"What were they doing?"

"Hunting big meat," answered Somah. "The woods are full."

Returning to his quarters, Jarbar found to his utter disappointment that Mr. Jackson's hunting equipment, ammunition, etc., were all missing. This confirmed what Somah had said. It was evident that the carriers had helped themselves and ventured far out in the dense woods to try their fortune with the dangerous and ferocious beasts which usually only old and intrepid hunters dare tackle.

"I begged them," said Somah, "not to go so far."

FOLK-LORE FROM AFRICA

Zindar voluntarily bore witness to Somah's entreaties with them, which had been in vain. "And," said Zindah, wildly staring, "leopards, elephants, boa constrictors, gorillas, baboons, monkeys, all live there too much."

"But," said Goo-ah, who also stood in the group, "one brave Bassa man go wid um, no fear!" and this furnished a ray of hope.

Suddenly a man came rushing in the town as if hotly pursued by a wild beast. He was panting as though well nigh exhausted; blood was trickling down his legs, where the briars and sword-grass had made sad havoc as he tore through the jungles beast-like.

"Who are you?" stormed Jarbar, his thoughts running riot over the fate of the boys.

The man was dumb. His frame trembled with emotion, and his lips quivered. His eyes stared in wild confusion, and his gestures were quick and nervous.

"Speak, man; speak!" shouted Jarbar; but again no word was uttered.

When finally he had recovered himself he began a series of frantic, unintelligible mutterings and grimaces, accompanied by savage-like gestures, pointing first to the trickling blood that ran down his bare legs and then in the direction of the big bush from whence he came. It was evident that

MISSIONARY STORY SKETCHES

the man was unable to speak in any other language save that of signs and groans, for he was dumb.

As quick as a flash the natives took in the whole drama. The boys had encountered some awful disaster with dangerous beasts far out in the wilds.

"Just what the details of the tragedy are," thought Mr. Jackson, "God only knows," when the news was communicated to him.

"They must be rescued," he said, "even at the peril of my own life."

In less time than it takes to tell it, the natives had formed a squad of men armed with guns, spears, bows and arrows, clubs, and war knives, headed by the king, who, though advanced in years, was as nimble as when in his young manhood he fought both savage beasts and men. Mr. Jackson and Jarbar accompanied them. The dumb man had already dashed ahead, so swiftly that at every turn and bend of the road only his rapidly moving legs could be seen.

On, on the crowd rushed through the deep, tangled forest. The sun was slowly setting, and whatever rescue was to be given must be done with haste, for the darkness of the night and the denseness of the forest would make conflict in the woods with wild animals exceedingly dangerous. Between them and the dreary distant spot lay streams and mountains.

"Come this shorter route!" shouted the king,

and the men went tearing through the bush behind him. The king's command recalled days of yore, when similar rescue parties scoured the forest to save distressed tribesmen.

Night came all too soon, and there was yet a long distance to travel. Darkness like a pall encompassed them, and they could make their way through the forest only by means of bamboo torches. Strange noises were heard from every side; falling trees, monkeys chattering, water dashing over rocks, elephants clumsily striding through the jungles, hippopotami playfully sporting among the reeds and rushes, winds whispering through the tall trees.

All night the rescue party pursued their way. Excitement nerved them, and weariness gave place to surprising strength as they drew nearer to the supposed place where the unfortunate carriers had strayed in their quest for game.

The dawn of morning was purpling the eastern horizon when the king whispered, "Hush!"

He crept stealthily in the tall, dangerous-looking grass, and with uplifted hand beckoned the men to remain where they were. He advanced alone a step or two farther toward the threatening jungles.

There, to his consternation, a scene met his gaze that caused his old heart to quake with fear and his firm hand to tremble; but, having faced similar dangers many times before, it was only momentary and, beckoning to his men to come to his assistance, he hastened on.

On the ground lay prostrate a huge female leopard, with a shoulder slashed open with a gash which extended halfway down her body. Upon her neck and head was stretched one of Mr. Jackson's carriers. He had exhausted his supply of ammunition in his efforts to kill the beast; but having had no experience with shooting leopards, had missed her in every shot but one, which had served only to enrage her, the more so that she had young ones near by to protect, and she had attacked him. He then resorted to his knife, and in the close combat managed to inflict the gaping wound, which had not, however, vitally injured the brute, though he saw by her loss of blood that if he could hold out long enough he could conquer her; but only in that way, for his knife had been flung from his reach in the struggle.

But the monstrous cat, as though determining that he should pay dearly for his prize, shook him from her back and sprang upon him with all the ferocity and strength of her vicious nature. With quick agility he sprang back, thus escaping instant death, and in the next moment man and beast were again in deadly combat, the snarls of the latter mingling with the heavy, gasping breathing of the former.

FOLK-LORE FROM AFRICA

Back and forth the two struggled, every second fraught with mortal peril to the carrier. The king dared not aim at the leopard, for, even had he been nearer, any such effort would have as probably killed the man as they writhed together.

On a low, projecting limb, broken at the end, of a nearby dead tree, a group of monkeys gathered curiously, then ran screaming and chattering in affright away, as the warring pair came foot by foot nearer them. At last, at the very foot of the tree the leopard stood almost upright upon her hind paws, and it seemed inevitable to the party, who at this moment reached the advancing king's side, that the man would at last meet his awful death from those foaming jaws and gnashing teeth, or those cruel forepaws.

Sickened by the sight, powerless to help, yet determined to at least try something, Mr. Jackson and the king simultaneously sprang forward, but suddenly stopped short with a united cry of wonder, for a passing strange and almost unbelievable happening terminated the battle.

The carrier, with a last gathering together of his wasted forces, half pushed, half flung the animal from him as she stood, and in so doing the exposed flesh just below the shoulder was forced against the very limb of the tree the monkeys had but a moment earlier vacated. The jagged, sharp end where the limb had broken embedded itself slantwise, and thus, as with a human deliberate aim, pierced the heart of the monster.

Even a last cry of agony could not escape the enraged victim as she fell, with a heavy thud, bearing with her a good portion of the dead wood, which snapped from the tree as she dropped, lifeless, beside the exhausted carrier.

"Come on!" thundered the king, who had paused in silent marveling; and it had all happened so quickly none were yet upon the spot. The sudden command frightened the man, who had been alone for hours and who was nervous from the awful strain of the battle he had just been through.

"Safe! Safe!" he cried, with a hysterical break in his voice.

A moment brought them to his side, and wild, prolonged shouts of joy made the forest ring as all beheld the triumphal scene. The man's body was crimson with his own blood and that of the beast, and his flesh was gashed open here and there, where the cruel paws had done their work. Cold water from the spring near by, and juices from the medicinal plants in the midst of which he had lain, did effective work as he was tenderly cared for.

The other men, they found, having been pursued by a drove of wounded elephants in the grassy plains near at hand, had fled in dismay, thus leaving their companion to his fate. They took a shorter route home and greeted the party on their return.

The leopard's flesh was put up in kinjars and borne to the town in triumph, where a feast followed. Her skin and teeth were given to Mr. Jackson as a souvenir of that memorable chase and a trophy of native valor.

CHAPTER XI

THE LEAVE-TAKING.—A LETTER.—A CLOSING WORD.

The next day at sunrise Mr. Jackson and his carriers took their leave of the old king and his people, amid mingled feelings of joy and sadness. The king, who had rejoiced at his coming, wept at his departure and was consoled only in the hope of his speedy return to live and work in his country.

As an expression of appreciation for the visit he presented a bullock to his guest, and three men to lead it all the way through the wilderness from Kie Tipoor to Monrovia, a distance of two hundred miles or more. When Mr. Jackson reached Monrovia, by the quickest possible route, the men had been awaiting him three days.

The king's and commissioner's communication to the president of the republic elicited the following reply:

EXECUTIVE MANSION, MONROVIA, LIBERIA,
15th April, 1907.

SIR: Referring to your project for the establishment of an Industrial Mission and School in the Gibi District, Grand Bassa County, I hasten to assure you that I heartily indorse the idea, and trust that you will get the necessary financial support in the United States and elsewhere for its successful initiation.

The government will grant 1,000 acres of land, and in addition will give all countenance and protection and such financial assistance as may be within its means.

I think the school should be planned on ample basis, so as to attract the attention of the heathen people among whom it is proposed to found it.

With heartiest desire for your success,
Yours faithfully,
(Signed) ARTHUR BARCLAY,
President of the Republic of Liberia.

Two days after his arrival in Monrovia, Mr. Jackson embarked for the United States. After an ocean voyage of three weeks he reached New York. He was warmly received by friends, who were greatly interested in the thrilling experience he here relates.

Upon hearing the gist of this story, "In Liberia's Wilderness and Beyond," friends thought it worthy of its present form. The leading threads from which the fabric of the story is woven are true; method, color, and art having been only moderately employed by the writer for literary effect and to improve the setting of the narrative.

It is the cherished hope of the author that the scheme of work proposed, namely, the establishment of an industrial school in the interior of Liberia, may receive such practical co-operation of friends

MISSIONARY STORY SKETCHES

of Liberia and Africa as shall make possible the speedy realization of that work, so that the thousands of pagan tribes in whose midst the school is to be planted, as well as those in the vaster regions beyond, may no longer be deprived of the blessings of civilization and enlightenment.

A WEST AFRICAN IDYL

Cool calm of evening had replaced the smoldering heat of the West African day, and the brazen glare of the sun had ceased, to be followed by the enchanting mellow light of the tropical moon. Utterly exhausted after the day's honest toil, we sat on the veranda of the mission house, enjoying one of those rare periods in our West African life.

The mail steamer had lately brought us good news and tender messages from the loved ones at home; and to add to our sense of joy, our little circle, which had so narrowly escaped being broken by the ravages of the virulent fever, was still intact, and the dear one who had for ten days hovered on the borderland of eternity had traveled back along the byways of earth again. And so we were silently enjoying a sense of fellowship, having reached that stage of congeniality when conversation is not at all necessary to express those deeper emotions of the soul, that state when silence is soothing, golden; knitting more closely the souls of those who have passed through some great crisis together.

MISSIONARY STORY SKETCHES

Thus we sat, gazing out across the moonlit landscape, our eyes focused on nothing in particular, until a dusky form obtruded itself upon our view, which, as it emerged from the scrubby bush that surrounded the little path leading down the mountain-side, gradually took the shape of a man. Evidently weary and footsore, he stumbled, rather than walked, toward the mission-house. He advanced slowly, with great difficulty, and reaching the house, he gasped, "O, daddy!—me—no fit—fer live," and sank to the ground, apparently lifeless.

"Call the boys and carry the poor man into the house," I said. "And, doctor, see what you can do for him," as I hastened down the veranda steps to give directions to the boys, who had come at our call from their dwelling hard by.

"Here, Walla, take him so; and Wah, lend a hand here!" Thus they carried the poor, stricken man into the house and laid him on a mat. In the meantime the doctor came up with his medicine case and bandages, having discerned that he had use for both. No clothing covered the ghastly wound across the shoulders, and his nude body bore here and there evidence of cruel torture.

"He is not dead," said the doctor, after a brief examination, "but nearly so from the loss of blood; there is scarcely a spark of life remaining."

Deftly and quickly the wound was dressed, and

FOLK-LORE FROM AFRICA

restoratives applied. Finally a faint sound, between a sigh and a moan, was emitted by the sufferer. Save this he gave no sign of life, but continued to lay inert, staring into vacancy.

The African natives, with their stalwart, athletic frames and iron constitutions, are noble specimens of physical manhood. And what possibilities there must be for a race for whom nature has done so much! The brawn and muscle of the African is his fortune. With these controlled by a cultivated and developed mind, he will rise in power and strength to the full accomplishment of his work and destiny on the continent. Thus we ruminated as we gazed upon this powerful form before us. Although intensely suffering from what would have been a mortal wound to many a civilized man, he would doubtless recover, with a little care and attention.

After administering to the various needs of the patient, the doctor installed Walla as attendant, with strict injunctions to notify him immediately of any signs of consciousness or need of extra attention. We then turned our faces again towards our dwelling. But the spell of the moonlight was broken, and curiosity regarding the poor fellow who so abruptly intruded upon our musings had taken possession of us. Each longed to say to the other, " Who is he?" "Where did he come from?" But each refrained, from some indefinable feeling of reluctance, to admit that he was curious about the strange moonlight visitor.

As we were not inclined to remain on the veranda, we separated for the night, each going to his own apartments. There was no summons during the night, but the doctor was up betimes the next morning to visit his patient. When we met at breakfast I could gain no idea of what the physician thought, from his inscrutable countenance. So I ventured to ask, "How is he?"

"To tell you the truth," blurted out the doctor, "I hardly know how he is. But this I can tell you: if he is one of those rum-guzzling natives, I would not give a fig for his chance of life with that great, ugly, gaping wound."

I wanted to say more regarding the man, but refrained, as the doctor had addressed himself to his breakfast with that vigor with which a man is likely to who rises at dawn and puts in several good hours of work before the first meal of the day.

After a prolonged pause I remarked, "I think I shall start up the country, for I am anxious to seal that compact with old King Donda about opening up that new station in his country, and I should like to take Walla with me."

The doctor shifted uneasily in his chair and said, "I wish you would postpone your trip until later, for, from the appearance of that fellow, I believe the natives are again on the warpath back there."

"What makes you think so?" I queried.

"Well," said the doctor, evasively, "I believe that fellow has a strange story to tell as soon as he can find his tongue; so wait at least a few days before you start."

So, thus advised, I acquiesced and, concluding our meal, we separated to our different tasks for the day. One of mine was to meet the bands of natives who came down from up the country to dispose of native produce, taking in trade cutlasses, pots, cloth, beads, etc. The doctor at the same time conducted a free dispensary.

I stepped out of the door and walked towards the palaver house, a building used for storage purposes, with an empty room on the ground floor wherein I received these deputations, talked trade with them, and transacted all matters of a business nature. There were two groups awaiting me this morning, lazily lounging against the veranda steps or squatting around the yard with their "kinjars" (baskets carried on the back) deposited at their feet, though still fastened to their backs.

I noticed nothing unusual about either of the groups as they chatted sociably together, except that one old man of dignified mien bore no burden and sat apart, seemingly ill at ease. He had in charge a buxom girl in early womanhood. The fact of the woman's presence was not in itself strange, for often both old women as well as young travel with these little bands of natives, many times bearing burdens on their heads as well as children on their backs. But I could not remember ever having seen either of these two before, though distinctly recalling the faces of all others of the group, as they were in the habit of frequenting the station.

As I made my way through the gathering the boys were filing out of the schoolhouse, whither they had been summoned by the bell from shop and farm to morning devotion. They were running and leaping with all the exuberance of young African life towards their mess hall, where plentiful plates of rice and palm butter awaited them. Across the river could be seen the girls as they, likewise, marched into their breakfast room.

The men fell in behind me as I proceeded toward the palaver house, and decorously arranged themselves in a line as I had taught them to do, as I insisted upon holding palaver with but one man at a time, thus expediting the tedious business.

To my surprise the old man, who seemed to have no business to transact, placed himself, with the woman, at the head of the line. Thinking he had mistaken me for the doctor, I spoke to him in English, pointing out to him at the same time the house where the doctor was then receiving his patients. He replied merely by shaking his head. So to the boy who usually helped me with these palavers I then said, "Ask him what tongue he understands." The boy put the question in several dialects common to that part of the country, and finally, after much questioning, received a reply in a dialect with which I was unacquainted, but which the boy defined as the Bassa-Gibi tongue. We finally managed to comprehend that the old man wished to be allowed to stay at the mission with the woman. When asked if she was his daughter, he answered, "No." His sister; "No."

Desiring to finish the task before me as soon as possible, in order that I might repair to that of schoolmaster, I requested the old man to step aside with the woman, and disposed of the rest of the persons in the line. When I finished with these, I told the boy to take the man and the girl to the mess-room and feed them, and bring them to me later in the day when I had more leisure. I then hastened to my duties in the schoolhouse, where the pupils had gathered.

The classes of the advanced scholars were being conducted in a large room apart from the smaller boys, who were intent at their books in their department. All the pupils were bending diligently over their tasks, and there was no sound except the busy hum of the subdued voices of the little boys, which in no way disturbed those who were used to it.

Suddenly the stillness was pierced by a shrill

MISSIONARY STORY SKETCHES

scream, which seemed to convey a world of agony and despair. The doctor came running from his dispensary, meeting Walla on his way to summon him, who explained, as they hurried along, that the woman, after leaving the mess-room, had wandered aimlessly into the room where the wounded man still lay almost dead. Upon beholding him she had for a moment stood as one transfixed with horror, then with that piercing scream which had attracted our attention she had thrown herself down beside the man in the utter abandonment of grief in which the natives often indulge. I placed a monitor in charge and accompanied the doctor to the scene of what I feared might be a tragedy; for I felt, from the doctor's demeanor at breakfast, that he had small hope for the man's life, and I feared lest the sudden shock might have snapped the slender thread.

When we reached the room where the wounded man lay, we found that his eyes no longer stared into vacancy; while his body lay inert, yet his eyes rested with tender recognition upon the woman who knelt sobbing and wailing by his side, and his hand was clasped lovingly in the hand of the old man, who, like we, had been attracted thither by the scream. Silently we looked upon this tableau for a moment, then, professionally alert, the doctor brusquely pushed aside the old man and the woman and made his way to the patient's side.

FOLK-LORE FROM AFRICA

Feeling his pulse and carefully examining him, he nodded his head satisfiedly and said briefly, "He will live."

"I feared the shock might be fatal to him," said I.

"Joy is a more potent healer than potions," was the rejoinder.

When his face lost its preoccupied look, and his jovial disposition again showed itself in his countenance, I knew that the doctor rejoiced that another soul had been snatched from the jaws of death, either by his skill or by that joy which he affirmed was more potent than pills and draughts.

The woman stoutly refused to leave the room, and at the least sign of coercion she bristled like a tigress defending her young. Seeing the situation, the doctor counseled leaving her with the patient. Little information could be had from the old man; but we were able to gather that the wounded man was his son, and the woman was his son's wife.

Anxiously we waited for the story which we were now doubly sure the injured man had to tell. True to the doctor's prediction, he recovered rapidly and in a few days "found his tongue," and this, briefly told, is the story he poured into our listening ears:

When a very young man he had married the girl according to the laws of his country and the custom of his tribe. It was not a case of buying a wife commercially, and living with her as is the custom in Africa; but he loved her with all the wealth and depth of affection possible to man. He desired to keep her as befitted an African lady. To do this he must purchase other women to work for her. These women, as viewed by native law and usage, are wives also, although they may sustain no marital relation.

In order that he might accomplish his ambition more quickly, he left the girl in charge of his father and made his way to the coast to ship on one of the steamers as a workman. Reaching Monrovia, he shipped with a gang of natives for this purpose. He was carried to Fernando Po, a West African Island belonging to Spain, and there engaged as a laborer for a number of years on the large plantations.

Natives thus hired are very cruelly treated by the overseers. They are made to drudge as slaves of former years in Africa. The treatment meted out to them is not unlike that given the natives in the basin of the Congo. Year after year thousands are killed, imprisoned, incapacitated, and subjected to brutalities and atrocities which no pen can describe. He attempted to break away, and for this he was bound and beaten unmercifully, and a close watch kept on him by the heartless guards.

After five years he succeeded in making his escape on a steamer calling at that port, secreting himself until he reached Lagos. From there he managed to ship with a humane captain, and worked his way back to Monrovia. Reaching this port he rapidly pushed his way back into the interior to his home.

In the meantime the woman's parents had sold her to another man, and she was compelled to leave her father-in-law from up the country, and arrived on the coast the following morning. Such was the history they told us.

On leaving the mission, a palaver soon followed in their country to adjust the entanglement and irregularities which had happened during the young husband's absence. These were very soon effected in the interest of the once wounded man, now thoroughly recovered and strong.

When a lad of tender years this young man had been placed in the mission by his heathen parents. He soon acquired the elements of an English education and made marked advancement in morals and industry. His training in these few years he never forgot, and although compelled to earn his living under circumstances anything but conducive to his mental and spiritual growth, he walked steadily in wisdom's way, earnestly seeking to live up to the light he had.

Not many days after the palaver had been settled, two parties found their way to the mission.

MISSIONARY STORY SKETCHES

Then was heard, floating on the balmy air, merry chimes of wedding bells. Jarlikar and Fembar in comely and simple dress stood before the altar, in the sight of God and in the presence of witnesses, to be joined in the bonds of holy matrimony in accordance with laws higher than those of their country and tribe—the laws of God.

AN AFRICAN GIRL'S STORY

TWILIGHT, short in its duration, was over; the sun seemed to drop into old ocean, and a somber darkness quickly settled upon the earth. Soon the stars appeared and shone with brilliant luster from the celestial heights, as under a huge Mango plum tree, with its stalwart and wide-spreading branches and myriad of leaves, Wanah sat, in deep meditation. On her face there was a far-away look of pity and sadness. One could see that her heart was deeply stirred and that her thoughts were from her inmost soul. Her schoolmates were about her, gayly romping, and their merry laughter and native songs rang out heartily on the evening air, but Wanah seemed oblivious of them.

Although a healthy and strong girl, and entering heartily into innocent play and fun, to-night she was quiet and almost melancholy. She was a typical African maid, with pronounced native fea-

FOLK-LORE FROM AFRICA

tures, and bearing the conspicuous tribal mark on her forehead. Having recently emerged from the darkness of paganism and been brought in contact with civilization, this new life was strange to her, and it was interesting to observe her as she entered into it, and what a striking contrast it presented to her former life and condition, and how grateful she seemed to be for her rescue; all of which was voiced most eloquently as she described in her artless way the pathetic story of her people.

As I sat there, watching her and thinking of God's goodness to her, and of His providential leading; of her consistent Christian life; of her high appreciation of the privileges she enjoyed and the fond hopes she cherished for better days for her people; I finally concluded to break the silence—a silence in which nature seemed to join—by speaking to her.

Accordingly I said in a cheery voice, "A penny for your thoughts."

She turned her winsome but sad brown eyes to me and, smiling, said, "I was thinking of my people far away in the Detebe country, and of how they suffer from ignorance, superstition, and witchcraft." She paused; but wishing to know more of her thoughts and more concerning her particular tribe, I prompted, "Have you been thinking of any particular incident?"

"Yes, and a very painful one to me—one in

which my own family was concerned, and which not only cost us our home, but a dear father too."

Again she paused, and for awhile sat in painful silence. Finally she volunteered, "Would you like to hear my story?" and upon receiving my affirmative answer, related the following sad tale:

"My father was rather a progressive man among his people and was not satisfied to sit around the palaver house all day long and talk, but he planted nice, large farms, raised goats and chickens, as well as cassavas, edoes, yams, and plenty of pepper. He did not compel mother to do all the work, but labored side by side with her. Although he was a heathen and believed sincerely in the traditions of his tribe and was in sympathy with most of the customs and practices, yet there were some of them he did not believe in and would not follow.

"Because he differed in many points with his tribesmen he was looked upon with suspicion, and men less thrifty envied him his good farm and the plenty he always had to eat. It was whispered among them that he must have a witch, and there was much curiosity as to what kind brought him such good luck. Father denied it, of course, but they would not believe him. And about this time an incident occurred that made them more suspicious than ever.

"About this time two missionaries came to our country and began Christian work about three days' walk, or about seventy-five miles, from our town. The news immediately spread among the surrounding tribes that there were women who had come to teach the people about the Great Spirit—Nyesoa. They were looked upon with wonder and amazement.

"My father left home one morning before the first peep of the pepper bird. He said nothing to any one as to where he was going, not even to mother. Two weeks passed, and then he returned and told my mother that he had been to see the strangers, the 'God women,' and the things they said and did pleased him very much. He also added that he had made up his mind to give his three daughters to the missionaries, that they might learn 'God way' and not grow up heathen fashion. My mother felt very sad and was quite unwilling to have us civilized; but father was determined, and would not listen to the prayers and entreaties of our mother.

"Early next morning found us stumbling along the narrow bush path. Our little sister was soon too tired to walk, but father took her on his back and we continued the journey, sleeping two nights by the wayside, until late in the afternoon of the third, when we reached the mission.

"We had never seen any one wearing clothes before, and it was a strange sight to us. However, when the lady spoke to me in my own tongue and

MISSIONARY STORY SKETCHES

asked of me if I were tired and had walked all the way, her kind face and gentle voice dismissed my fear of her appearance and soothed my aching heart, for I must confess I was heart-sore over the thought of leaving mother and the scenes I had known and loved so well all of my young life.

"The missionary called one of the mission girls and told her about us. We were then conducted to the country kitchen, where we saw a number of girls of all sizes and were given a large bowl of rice and palm butter, which we very much enjoyed, for the long walk had sharpened our appetites and we were very hungry. After our first meal in the mission was over we went to the creek running at the back of the grounds, and, taking off our dress, which was a few yards of cotton material, we plunged into the cool, clear stream and bathed our tired limbs.

"Very soon we heard a sound such as we had never heard before. Instantly all the girls were on shore, dressed, and hastening toward the quarters from whence the strange music, as I thought, came. It was the evening prayer bell calling the mission children to prayer. I took each of my sisters by the hand, and we all joined the company, as we were bidden by one of the girls, in prayer.

"I remember very distinctly that first evening in the mission. I was too frightened to be sleepy;

everything was strange to me. I had never heard the singing of Christian songs before, and I felt like running away, when one of the ladies went to the organ and began to make it cry, as I thought. However, I was too tired to run; therefore I sat still upon the floor, in ignorance as to what it all meant. The children sang, the evening lesson was read; but not a word do I remember hearing that night except the word 'Jesus.' The lady told us about Him, and the children sang the touching hymn, which I have since learned and love, 'Yes, Jesus loves me.'

"My father was present, and I could tell from the expression on his face that he was much pleased. After the meeting was over he took us by the hand and told the missionary that he gave us to her to make 'God women' of us, and that he never wanted us to return to heathenism again. She said she would do her best for us; then father placed our hands in hers. We were then given a mat, and I cried myself to sleep, as did my other sisters. The next day father was gone; nor did we hear from, nor see, him and mother for a long time.

"Nearly five years had passed since we entered the mission, when one morning early our Christian mother, as we had learned to call the missionary (there was only one left, as the other had died the year before of African fever), sent for me and said, 'Wanah, your father has sent for you and your sisters, and desires you to come home at once.'

"I fell on my knees and buried my head in her lap and wept aloud. I knew that there was only one thing to do, for only one thing would cause my father to take such a step. Some palaver had caught him, and according to our tribal custom all the family must be present when the palaver was held, and they perhaps share in the punishment. After comforting me all she could, and placing a New Testament in my hand, bidding me seek comfort and guidance therein, we started on our three days' journey.

"Upon our entering the town we were taken to the palaver house, and there we found father a prisoner in 'sticks.' Perhaps you do not know what I mean by 'sticks?' A log about four feet long and twelve inches in diameter is cut from a tree, and a hole just large enough to force one foot through is made, and both feet are forced through. This is very painful, and many times the feet become swollen, and the misery is very great.

"We were allowed to greet father, and mother, who was also present, and were compelled to remain in the palaver house all night, as our own house and belongings had been confiscated and were in the hands of the soldiers. Early next morning people from the town and from other towns came to hear the palaver talked. The king's head carrier had died, and my father was accused of witching him and causing his death. Father declared his innocence; hence this trial.

"Three days' palaver concluded against my father, and it was decided to subject him to punishment until he should confess. Accordingly his farm was burned, his cattle eaten, and his hut plundered. They threatened to sell mother and us children. I can not yet tell you all the wicked punishment they put father to to make him confess. Finally they put him in the smoke-house of punishment, which is a small hut closely built of mud walls and thatch covering.

"Father was taken to this hut and placed up in the loft about eight or ten feet from the fire. Logs were placed in the middle of the dirt floor and a fire started. Then everything, such as leaves, damp bark of trees, etc., was placed on this fire to make a nasty smoke, and, to add to the suffering, handfuls of pepper were thrown on. This agony is very intense, and many times victims confess to crimes they have never committed to escape punishment. The cruel ordeal was kept up for hours, but father could not confess to that which he had not done. When he was taken out he was more dead than alive, and was never thereafter able to look upon the beauties of nature, for he was stone-blind. It was of this I was thinking, and it made me feel sad."

"What became of your mother and father after this, and how did you get back to the mission?"

"O, mother and the children were sold, and father, poor father, could not long survive such cruelty, and within a short time died. But before he left us he called me to him and said: 'Wanah, I want you to promise me by all we hold sacred and dear that you will not grow up a heathen and perhaps have to suffer as I have; but take your sisters and run away to the mission, and there remain until you are grown. Then return to your tribe and be a "God woman" for them.' Father spoke with emphasis at first, but his voice growing fainter, he whispered: 'O, Wanah! our people are in darkness, and they need light. Help them, Wanah, my child!'

"He drew his knife from his sheath, placed it to his lips, then reached out his arm, extending it to me. I placed my lips thereon and solemnly promised to keep this pledge. That night, with my youngest sister tied on my back and the other's hand in mine, we started for the mission. We traveled by night and hid in the bush by day until the journey was ended.

"My father died within a month after receiving intelligence of our safe arrival at the mission.

FOLK-LORE FROM AFRICA

Messengers brought us word. They said he died faintly whispering the word he learned to love so well, 'Jesus.' It was several years before we saw our mother again. I am glad to say that her brother's town was her last home, for he learned where she was and went to her rescue, and she still lives there."

Years have passed since Wanah related this pathetic story of her family life. She and her sisters are now developed into beautiful Christian characters and are seeking, in their humble sphere as native helpers far out amid the wilds of nature and the darkness of heathenism, to carry out the last request of their father; and the Father above, who faileth not to take knowledge of a single sparrow so that no one falleth on the ground without His notice, looks down with tender love upon these humble toilers, and their ministrations in His name are not unnoticed nor unrewarded.

LOST AND FOUND

"Good-bye, ma! Do n't cry, for I shall soon come back to you," said little Zoe-jar, as she stood in the doorway, waving one hand and holding in the other a little piece of blue denim containing a change of clothing.

She smiled sweetly as she said the parting

word; but Mrs. Brown, the good mother of the mission home, tried hard to restrain the tears that forced themselves down her cheek, for somehow she felt that Zoe-jar was slipping from her hands, and perhaps she would never see her again. Her parents, who were heathen people, had been to the mission several times to ask permission to take her to their home, about seventy-five miles away, that she might see her grandmother and a host of other relations, who mourned her as dead and would not believe that she lived unless they could see her face to face.

Six years before our narrative begins, the people of the Golah district and the Mandingo people had fought a bloody war; the Mandingoes were victors and drove the Golahs from their towns and half towns; devastated their lands, burned their huts, captured their cattle, and carried away and destroyed their foodstuffs, thus compelling the Golahs to flee in confusion for their lives.

The native warrior is pitiless on the warpath, and "their tender mercies are cruel." Many of the women, with their babies strapped to their backs, who could not get out of the way, were either killed outright or captured and doomed to a far worse fate—slavery. Old King Zingby was called the lion of the wood, and it was said that the flash of his eye caused his enemies to run and lose themselves in the depths of the forest. Such

FOLK-LORE FROM AFRICA

was his barbarity that he spared neither age nor sex; the suckling child shared the fate of its mother, and the unfortunates begging for mercy fell as the vanquished in battle.

So fierce was the conflict and great the suffering of the unfortunates that the Liberian Government sent relief parties to rescue the unforunate wanderers in the African jungles who were without food and shelter save such as is to be found in the dense forest land. Among the first ones rescued was little Zoe-jar; she and her mother and brother had escaped from their town and were wandering about in the forest, hiding in the dense undergrowth, starting at every sound.

Hockbar, the mother, became tired, weary, and foot-sore, until she felt she could go no farther; and so she took from her arm her fetich and put it upon little Zoe-jar and said to her, "Run on, my child, and try to reach Suewah; for it may be that you may find friends there who will care for you, and you can bring help to me and Darkannah."

The weary woman turned aside from the weather-beaten path and sat down to rest, while the little girl ran down the pathway, hoping to reach the relief station and procure assistance for her mother and brother. Not knowing the way exactly, and coming to a place where several paths met, she took the wrong one, and for six weeks she was lost in the bush. When she was exhausted from hunger and tramping she crawled under the thick, tangled bush and lay down to sleep. It was thus the soldiers found her and took her to the camp, where she received food and clothing and found herself among friends. There were several hundred refugees, mostly children, already there.

The question that now confronted the authorities was, what to do with these unfortunate creatures. Their towns were burned, farms destroyed, parents killed—in fact, they could not be sent back to their country, for it was in the hands of the enemy; nor were they able to care for themselves. It was therefore decided to put the children in the Christian missions and to find homes for the older ones among the civilized folk or friendly natives.

They went to all of the missions near by and asked assistance in caring for the children. Mrs. Brown's mission was among the number, and, although she already had a very large family of native children and had no means of support for any more, she, being a woman of large faith and tender sympathy, and not liking to see such an opportunity for doing good pass, sent word that she would take one child. This child was our little friend Zoe-jar.

It was mid-afternoon when she was brought to Mrs. Brown's mission. Everything was new and strange to the child of the forest. She had never seen a house before, and it was with difficulty that she allowed herself to be persuaded to ascend the steps, which she did on her hands and knees; nor could she be coaxed to rise to her feet after she reached the little veranda along the front of the mission house. The good woman reached down and took the little girl in her arms and assured her that she was among friends. The little body, clothed only as Nature dresses her children, except for the fetich on her arm and a girdle of beads around her waist, was covered from head to foot with scratches and wounds she had received by the tall sword-grass and dragon blood strewn in her path. She was an object of pity, and Mrs. Brown's heart was deeply stirred as she folded this child of the bush in her arms.

Kindly care was given her and she was clothed in a simple garment. After a few days the strangeness of everything seemed to wear away and she began to show herself bright and helpful. She soon learned to do little tasks about the home, to read, write, cook, wash, and sew. Her chief delight seemed in being as quick and helpful as possible always, and she was especially fond of reading and sewing.

One day as she and Mrs. Brown sat alone in the little room that was used as a sewing-room, she said, "Ma" (in this manner all the children and many of the old folks addressed Mrs. Brown), "what is it to be a Christian? What do you mean by conversion?"

Mrs. Brown tried to explain in the simplest way the new birth, and summed up by saying, "To love God with all your heart, and your neighbor as yourself, seeking at all times to know His will and to do it."

"Ma, dear," said Zoe-jar, "I am converted."

"Every one who is converted knows it," said Mrs. Brown.

"Yes, ma; I know I am converted, because I love everybody," continued Zoe-jar. "I love those people who burned our farms and destroyed our huts; who killed our people without pity as they found them fleeing along the roads or in the towns. I would that I could tell them about this great God, who loves even Golah people.

"Do you know, ma, our people do n't know about Jesus? They know nothing about Sunday. They work on Sundays the same as any other day, making fish baskets, cutting palm nuts and making oil, planting rice, and working on the farm. When I am a woman I am going back to get all the children I can and teach them this little hymn, 'Yes, Jesus loves me, for the Bible tells me so.' I am going to have a little Sunday-school."

The good mother of the mission was greatly moved by this beautiful and spontaneous confes-

FOLK-LORE FROM AFRICA

sion of faith by this little child only a few years removed from heathenism. As soon as she could control her voice she said: "Yes, dear, mother wants all of her girls and boys to be Christian missionaries to their own people when they are old enough. You were brought to this Christian home to make preparation for just such work, and the Lord will bless you as you bless and make others happy."

Mrs. Brown then fell in a deep study as she thought of what the future held for this little one who was lost in the bush, who was not only found and rescued from the cruel ravages of the wild beast of the forest and more cruel hand of the enemies of her people; but who was redeemed of the Lord Jesus, of whose love she could testify.

When this little waif of the wilds was brought to Mrs. Brown she might have had fifty as easily as she took this one, if she had only had the means of maintenance for them. What a little army they would have been against the stubborn and contending forces of heathenism!

It has been several years since this incident occurred. Zoe-jar has returned to the mission from the visit to her people; she is now about fifteen years of age, and has the same desire to go among her people and help lift them up to Him who said, "And I, if I be lifted up from the earth, will draw all men unto Me;" also, "Come unto Me all ye that labor and are heavy laden, and I will give you rest."

Africa is rich and abundant in children. This is one of its brightest stars of hope, if Christendom would do its full duty in gathering them in from the wilds of nature and heathenism into the fold of Christ. Millions of little lambs like Zoe-jar are lost in the thickets of heathen Africa, only waiting the tender Shepherd's care. Zoe-jar's transformation shows the possibilities that lie buried beneath the rough and crude native material which may be refined and made polished stones for the building of our God.

Reader, suffer a personal word. What is your vision of the field? Is it broad or limited? Do you take in your view all men of whatever race, clime, or nation? Do you confine yourself to local interests or to those as broad as the kingdom itself? If from your heart and hand no help has gone for the uplift of God's humble poor in Africa, I bid you ponder the words of Sacred Writ and their far-reaching scope. "Ask of Me, and I shall give Thee the heathen for Thine inheritance, and the uttermost parts of the earth for Thy possession." "Say not ye, there are yet four months, and then cometh harvest; behold, I say unto you, lift up your eyes, and look on the fields; for they are white already to harvest."

FOLK-LORE FROM AFRICA

"WHAT WHITE MAN MAKE IT FOR?"

STENTORIAN in its tones, the voice of a stalwart native sang out gayly in his native vernacular as he deftly paddled his canoe up a Liberian stream. The stately palms and sasswoods, the tangled bamboos and other shrubbery, with their luxuriant foliage characteristic of the tropics, presented a beautiful picture, for the prismatic hues of the slanting rays of the morning sun were reflected on leaf and blade. The odor of fragrant flowers and water lilies permeated the air made sweeter by the songs of birds as they caroled in their leafy haunts.

But none of these beauties of nature appealed to the native, for his mind was preoccupied with a matter of far greater importance than the panorama nature had spread out before him. The song died away, and the man's brow grew thoughtful as he surveyed the contents of his canoe; and now he paddled more slowly, seemingly lost in meditation. Presently he plied his paddle more swiftly and sent the canoe skimming over the water like a bird in the air.

Deftly he paddled on until a bend in the river suddenly revealed the smoke curling up from the huts of a town not far in the distance. At this juncture he again relaxed his efforts, slowly paddled up into a little cove near at hand, and disembarked, taking from his canoe a cask, which he deposited upon the ground at his feet with several satisfactory grunts. Having made fast the canoe, he rolled the cask some distance from the river bank, and with the means of a sharp stick he proceeded laboriously to dig a hole, into which he deposited the cask. He then sought to remove all traces of the fresh dirt, taking care, however, to cut a notch in the tree near by to mark the spot. Returning to his craft, he proceeded on his journey to the town.

Dilema was a civilized (?) native. He was as sharp in trade as any son of Abraham, and as vicious as the bad examples of the traders and the brutalizing effects of New England rum and Holland gin could possibly make him. His constant mingling with that class of men who, having thrown off all restraints of home and civilization, are little more than savages themselves, and his frequent potations had transformed him from the ordinarily harmless, good-natured native of West Africa into a sordid wretch, who cared for nothing but the gains his transactions brought him.

He was a well-known personage in all the country towns and half towns within a radius of a hundred miles, for he was a rum agent for the firm of Messrs. N. & G., at Y——, dealers in African produce. His method of disposing of his ware was to convey it to a place near where he was going to trade, conceal it so that the natives might not know how much he had, make his bargains, then produce it as part payment for the produce, sometimes giving it as whole payment; thus the wretched stuff was distributed among the people, binding them with bands stronger than iron and sinking them lower and lower in degradation and misery.

Upon this occasion Dilema knew that the great heathen dance and festival was near at hand, and that rum would be one of the principals in the celebration of the "country devil." He also knew that it would be procured at any cost. So the firm in question dispatched their worthy agent to the town with a goodly supply of rum and a few other articles of trade. The carriers proceeded on foot, but Dilema preferred the shorter water route and to carry the rum himself.

Upon his arrival at the town he was greeted with a welcome by the inhabitants, who knew full well that he had brought with him plenty of the craved fluid. He began to disperse petty presents among them, and quite captivated the women and children by his generosity, giving to one a string of beads, to another a bright piece of cloth, and such like. It took but little "palaver" to make bargains for the skins, rubber, ivory, palm kernels,

MISSIONARY STORY SKETCHES

piassava, etc., which the natives brought for his inspection, and the shrewd fellow took care to get the best of every bargain for himself. He departed ostensibly to meet his carriers, but in reality to conduct them to the place where he had buried the cask to fill the numerous demijohns they were to bring with them. There was the usual uproar, so characteristic of the West African natives, when the carriers arrived, for the pleasant prospect of a big dance and plenty of rum was to them now an assured reality.

An interval of a few days, and then the strange scratchy sound of the kitty-katty, the indescribable noise of the tom-tom, the toot-toot-toot of the ivory horn, the deep boom-boom of the African drum, is borne upon the wind, mingled with the most unearthly cries, piercing shrieks, emphatic howls, and pathetic wails of men, women, and children as they frantically dance the "country" dance around the hoary-headed and besotted king, who sits like a specter in their midst. To the ear of a civilized mortal it would sound as though Pan and all the hordes of the Plutonian regions were let loose upon the earth. The poisonous beverage is quaffed as often as the old tin, which serves as a drinking-cup, is passed around. The women, poor creatures, drink of and transmit the foul stuff to the mouths of the babes at their breast, whose wails

FOLK-LORE FROM AFRICA

and piteous cries, as the fiery liquid burns into their tender pores, mingle with the demoniacal howls and senseless laughter of the elders.

As dawn begins to lighten the morning, at last worn out by exertion and stupefied by rum, the dancers lay prostrate around their king, who is stark and rigid in their midst—old men and old women, young men and young women, as well as children—stretched their full length upon the ground.

This was the result of one cask of rum shipped by some Christian (?) firm in civilized Europe or America to the dollar-grasping traders of West Africa. The liquor traffic of Africa is an appalling sin. It is a great curse resting on the continent like a horrid nightmare. African slavery with its score of unspeakable inhumanities had its modifying features. The poor African stolen from his country and torn away from his native shores against his will, crowded in the unsanitary hold of the slavers and brought across the high seas to labor for strangers, to have his life made bitter with hard bondage, might, if he would, on hearing the story of the cross, cast off the chains of darkness and be free in soul, if not in body. But this monster, this demon Drink, enslaves soul and body and damns both alike.

It is no exaggeration to say that there exists

no greater enemy to Africa and her people than this debasing evil inflicted by Christian nations. There is no greater obstacle to the progress of civilization and Christianity in Africa than this insidious foe, which is spreading desolation and ruin, despoiling Africa and destroying vigorous manhood and womanhood.

"What white man make it for?" is the unanswerable query the poor heathen invariably makes as he comes to himself, recovers his senses from his drunken stupor and revelries, and sees the awful wreck made by rum upon his unfortunate brethren. Why, indeed, may we ask, do civilized nations send missionaries to the heathen in Africa, and in the same ship send tons of brutalizing and soul-destroying rum to sink the African to still lower depths of sin and shame?

Africa in her dire necessities is calling loudly for bread—the Bread of Life—but a stone is given; she pleads pathetically for fish, but a fiery serpent, whose poisonous fangs strike deep in her bosom, is offered. Can we wonder, then, that even the blind, far-away heathen should ask a reason for that which is ruining him completely?

O, that the conscience of Christian Europe and America may be aroused to a sense of this awful wrong, and make haste to cease committing it!

FOLK-LORE FROM AFRICA

WHAT BECAME OF AN AFRICAN WITCH BABY

"This is a good time for you to tell me how you succeeded in getting such a bright girl as Bolah in the mission," said Miss Smith, the newly arrived missionary, to Mrs. Baker, who had charge of the station. Miss Smith had reached the West Coast only six weeks previously, and for the last fortnight had been confined to bed with an attack of African fever, which had abated considerably under the influence of large and frequent doses of quinine. She was slowly recovering and was able to sit up this day for the first time.

"I shall be delighted to do so if it will not tire you too much; it is a long story," said Mrs. Baker.

"I am quite sure it will be a pleasure rather than a taxation," replied Miss Smith, with a show of enthusiasm.

"Well," began Mrs. Baker, "it has been rather difficult to keep Bolah, but I do feel so thankful that we have a hold upon her. You know that the native people are very superstitious, believing in witchcraft and all sorts of voodooism. Nothing, they believe, ever happens without a supernatural cause; but they attribute every ill and evil that befalls them to the influence of some person. In the case of any sickness or death they believe that the enemies of the victim have bewitched them and caused their misfortunes.

"So it was in the case of this child's mother, whose name was Yeddo. Yeddo was the fifth wife of her husband, called Zinbar, who was by no means a young man. Zinbar fell sick, became steadily worse, until he finally died. We knew that his illness was the result of a diseased body, and that his death was the natural end; but, as I said, the natives will not credit things to natural causes. To make a long story short, Yeddo was accused of bewitching him and of being the cause of his illness and death. The young woman was filled with consternation when her accusers came to her hut and almost dragged her out to the palaver house.

"While she had not particularly cared for Zinbar, yet she had willingly accepted her fate, as is the case with thousands and thousands of African women who are sold to men without the least preference as to their wishes. She had been contented and had gone about her daily duties working on the rice farm, cutting wood, bringing water, making palm oil, and serving Zinbar whenever it was her turn. There had been no love, but there had been obedience and service such as expected of her. But somehow the rest of the family got it in their minds that she bewitched the old man."

"What reason had they for such suspicion?" interrupted Miss Smith.

"Well, no reason at all, unless it might have been jealousy; for Yeddo was a very handsome woman, as you can see by her child, who is very much like her mother. Anyway, they accused her, and she was compelled to undergo the usual test, although she protested her innocence, saying that neither while she slept nor yet when awake had she done such a thing, for Zinbar was always kind to her. You know, dear, so superstitious are these poor people that they believe there are times when the spirit wanders away from the body and gets into mischief, and at such times deeds are committed which they are unaware of. Yeddo's accusers said she must undergo the test of drinking sasswood, which would 'talk' for her, proclaiming her guilt or innocence."

"What is sasswood?" asked Miss Smith.

"Sasswood," said Mrs. Baker, "is the poisonous bark from the sasswood tree. They take this bark and boil it until they have a strong decoction, which is put in a vessel and placed in the center of the palaver house. After much deliberation on both sides by both the friends of the accused and accuser, the victim, who has been sitting silently by, rises up at the proper time and drains the vessel of its deadly draught. They believe that the poison will not affect them if they are innocent; but, of course, we know better.

"Yeddo drank the sasswood, dregs and all, to prove her innocence, but she soon staggered and fell forward—dying. Her enemies were loud in their accusations, and the shout that went forth from them as the unfortunate woman staggered and fell in terrible agony is a sound that I wish I could forget. Yeddo's three-months-old baby was tied upon her back as she drank the sasswood. Some of her friends took the child away as she lay writhing in agony upon the ground. Her body was dishonored, nor would they allow her to be buried near the town; her hut was burned, and her people were driven away.

"Three weeks later, while passing through the town, I saw a baby that looked starved and ill. I asked with what they were feeding it; and they said, 'Water.' They would take any kind of cloth, indifferent to how soiled it was, dip it in water, and squeeze it in the child's face. That the liquid went in the eyes, nose, and ears, little mattered; and what happened to find its mouth was what the babe had to subsist upon. I saw that the child could not long survive such treatment, and therefore I asked the woman who seemed to have charge of it to give it to me to take to the mission, where I would care for it.

"She readily consented, saying, 'O, it is a

witch child, and will die anyhow; and I would rather have it die in your house than in mine.' Pointing to it contemptuously, she concluded, 'Take it.' I took the little thing to the mission more dead than alive, but plenty of milk and kindly care soon worked wonders, and our witch baby began to grow.

"Years passed, and no one ever came to inquire about the child, until two years ago we had a message from the grandfather, Yeddo's father, saying that he was getting very old and was ill, and would like to see the child of his Yeddo. I had been expecting this, for Bolah was then a promising girl of twelve, old enough to be sold to some man for his wife, according to their custom. I therefore sent the messenger back to Fambah to say to him I regretted that he was so old and ill, but the journey was too long for so young a child as Bolah, and therefore she could not come.

"But with the pertinacity of the natives, who never give up easily when once they get started, he sent back several times. I knew he would not cease to annoy me, so planned to outgeneral him. When the next messenger came, I told him to go back to Fambah and tell him that I heard all he said, and would consent to let Bolah go to see him providing he would send me two of his young wives to hold as a pledge of good faith between us, I to return them when he returned Bolah to the mission. He said in reply to my proposition that my head was hard and that I had sense 'for true.' However, he sent the two young women. He felt that if he could only get Bolah into the town, her people would so influence her that she would run away from the mission and return to the native town. I felt equally sure that she would never allow herself to be persuaded to do such a thing. On the other hand, she might do some good among her people by her temporary visit to them. Fambah sent the two women, or girls, rather, and Bolah went with the messen

"Upon her retur .e told me many of her experiences while at ge-bo, her grandfather's town. Among other things she said that whenever they ate their meals they threw a generous portion in a little thatched apartment adjoining the living-room, in which was kept an ugly wooden idol, their family god, to which they made sacrifices. Her old Aunty Timba said to her one day, 'You give nothing to Coo; you keep all for your greedy self,' and threatened to punish her by rubbing pepper in her eyes, ears, nose, and mouth if she did not give something to the idol. Knowing that her aunt would carry out her threat, Bolah after this threw in a small portion, although it was distasteful to her to do so. She said, 'I know that piece of wood can not eat; but the ants and chickens had a good feast, as well as the dogs straying that way.'

FOLK-LORE FROM AFRICA

"After some time had passed she said to them: 'We don't do that way in the mission. We place our food on the table and sing:

> ' "God is great and God is good,
> And we thank Him for this food.
> By His hand must all be fed;
> Give us, Lord, our daily bread.
> Amen." '

"Bolah took with her an illustrated Testament and a little book of gospel hymns. Several weeks after her arrival she said to her people who had gathered around her, 'Let me tell you what my little book says,' and then she opened her Testament and began to read to them in the dialect of her tribe the story of redeeming love. She read on and on, one selection after another, until she reached that beautiful passage in St. John's Gospel which reads, 'For God so loved the world that He gave His only begotten Son, that whosoever believeth in Him should not perish, but have everlasting life.'

"Old Fambah threw up his hands imploringly and said: 'Stop, stop! Don't read any more of that God palaver to me, for you almost make me believe what you say is true. Where I a younger man I would believe in your God; but I am too old now. Too long have I believed in "devil doctors," witchcraft, charms, and ju-jus to give them up now.'

MISSIONARY STORY SKETCHES

"Bolah, continuing, said: 'I wish you would accept our Christ, grandpa. Although you are old, yet Christ will receive you if you turn from evil ways and seek Him.' Fambah made no reply to Bolah's entreaties; but Timba said: 'I should like to know this man Jesus, for He is not like any man I ever heard of. We have no men like Him in our tribe.' Then Bolah took up her little hymn book containing a collection of English and native hymns and sang with much feeling and beauty the following, her people joining in the chorus:

" ' 'T is so sweet to trust in Jesus,
    Just to take Him at His word,' etc.

" ' Come to Jesus just now,' etc.

" ' Blessed assurance, Jesus is mine,'

" ' *A muo klo be yu ti nyena
    A neo naye so ba bla.*'
    (We shall stand before the King.)

" ' *Mma kwie n kboi Grepaw,
    Mma kwie n kboi.*'
    (Nearer my God, to Thee.)

"Her sweet voice rang out melodiously, and the people in the neighboring huts were drawn to the music as she sang one hymn after another. Soon half the people in the town had gathered around her. Some who heard believed. All were

FOLK-LORE FROM AFRICA

melted to tears and trembled with emotion under the influence of these Christian songs that Bolah sang with such telling effect.

"When she returned to us her brother Daby came with her and has remained here ever since. The two girl wives, Mira and Zana, went home to the bush country, but were never satisfied there again after having spent two months in our mission home. When old Zinbar died, these girls ran away and came back to us, and we have kept them ever since. Of course, we have had to make returns to the family for them, but we were glad to do so, for the girls were worthy of all we could do for them.

"And that, dear, is all the story of Bolah that is so far written on the pages of her earthly life; but, as you have noticed, she is so bright and so loving that we have every reason to hope the completed story will make a beautiful volume before the Divine Author pens 'The End' in it."

CAUGHT IN THE SPIDER'S WEB

PANAH was a little girl living in the jungles of Africa, colloquially spoken of as the "bush" country. Her home was a thatch hut built of bamboo and daubed with clay and was one of a cluster of such abodes known as Pahboolah's town, beautifully situated at the foot of a range of high hills extending for miles away in the distance. In the forest around were trees of towering height and massive proportions, with foliage of every hue of green, from its deepest to its lightest tints.

The town was barricaded; a sort of native "walled city," composed of an inner and an outer wall of solid timbers pointed at the top and extending twelve feet in height. The timbers were so laid as to make the structure an impregnable parapet against attacks of the enemy. A stream, whose placid course was arrested by immense masses of rocks, wended its way by the side of the successive hills, and finally, gurgling down to a precipice of fifteen or twenty feet, fell over it and broke with violence on a second bed, emptying its waters at last into a river that found its way to the great ocean. In the midst of these wilds of the interior, with its tropical forest teeming with luxuriant vegetation, lived this little lass, an artless product of nature.

During the hours of the day Panah played in the open air, with its bright sunlight, and at night slept on the straw mat inside the rude shelter that composed her home. She was a bright-eyed, brown-skinned little girl, as plump as a partridge, and a fine row of pearly teeth showed themselves when she laughed, as she frequently did in her play. She was happy all the day long and a great favorite with the other children of the town in which she lived.

Her mother and father were justly proud of her and often "dashed" Tando, the country devil, in order that he might not vent his spite upon her. She wore numerous charms to ward off evil spirits and disease. Whether these served the purpose for which they were intended or not, Panah kept well and grew up into sturdy girlhood straight as an arrow and comely in appearance.

Kufi, a great warrior of the tribe and the chief adviser of the king, who already had a score of wives, offered to buy Panah for one. Her father consented, but told him she was too young to go with him to his hut then, and that he must wait until she had been in the Gri-Gri Bush and come out. Kufi paid the girl's dowry, and "dashed" the parents in addition.

Shortly after this Wamba and Ama, Panah's father and mother, took her and made a journey to the coast to do some trading. In the little town where they stopped a missionary held meetings every Sunday, and curiosity to hear what the "God man" was saying led Wamba into the little church house. The hymns that were sung in his own tongue made an impression upon him, and he began to think upon them. The more he pondered the more he was impressed, and he resolved to see the "God man" and hold "palaver" with him about the things he had been listening to. Accordingly he sought an interview. As the simple story of the cross always charms and draws men, so it affected Wamba; consequently he remained a longer time in the town than he might otherwise have done, to hear about this wonderful God. His conception of God had not been that of a kind, loving Father who delights to protect His children and to make them happy. Such a God as this appealed to him and filled a long-felt want in his nature. The next Sunday found Wamba at the little church house again, accompanied by Ama and Panah, and when service was over he sought again an interview with the missionary, telling him that he wished to know more about God, and that he wished Ama and Panah to learn about Him also.

The missionary told them as simply as he could about God's love for His children, and how He gave His own Son to die for man's sin that he might become reconciled to God. Wamba listened with intense interest, and declared that henceforth he would "live for God." The missionary asked that Panah be allowed to attend the mission school, and Wamba consented, although he remembered that she had been promised to Kufi for his wife. So Panah was left at the mission, Wamba and Ama returning home.

Kufi's indignation know no bounds when he learned that Panah had been left at the mission;

FOLK-LORE FROM AFRICA

he at once set about devising plans whereby he might gain possession of her. He hastened to the king and told him that he had "dashed" Wamba for his daughter, and he had carried her away. The king sent and called Wamba to a "palaver." Wamba told the king how he had been impressed by what the missionary told him about God, and ended by telling them of his resolve to "live for God" and have Panah stay at "God man's school to learn book" and become "God woman." The earnestness with which he spoke impressed all present, and it was decided that Kufi must wait until Panah returned to her parents.

This verdict did not pease Kufi by any means. He now began to plan the destruction of Wamba, who seemed to find untold pleasure in his new-found faith. He told Kufi that he intended to make another trip to the coast shortly to see and talk with the "God man" again; and when Kufi offered to accompany him, he gladly assented, not suspecting any treachery. The night before they were to start Kufi invited Wamba to his hut, where he and his companions were feasting, and Wamba accepted the invitation. Great was the merriment, for Kufi saw to it that there was plenty of rum.

The native African learns the vices of American and European civilization before he learns the virtues, and rum finds its way farther interior-ward than missionaries. Wamba refused to partake of the rum, and Kufi pressed upon him some palm wine, which he drank. Suddenly Wamba showed signs of illness and, before many moments, was in great agony. All declared that he was "witched," and forthwith the witch doctor was summoned to minister to the sick man and to discover the culprit. Before he arrived, however, Wamba was dead. Great was the commotion throughout the town when this fact became known. When she heard it, Ama hastened to the place where her husband lay dead.

In the meantime the witch doctor had arrived and was holding his mysterious incantations over the body. Spying Ama as she presented herself before the hut, wailing, he cried out that she who stood before the door was the culprit. Immediately she was seized and bound. Wamba was buried with great pomp and ceremony, with the firing of guns and dancing and drinking. Afterwards a council was held to determine the punishment of Ama. She was sentenced to drink the sasswood; in vain she protested her innocence, and entreated them to release her. She was only one more victim to Kufi's perfidy.

Kufi now determined to get possession of Panah at all hazards, and accordingly he presented himself at the school as her uncle and demanded her surrender. Panah denied the relationship and refused to go with him, and upon this ground the missionary refused to give her up. Kufi threatened and entreated, but to no effect; finally he left, saying he would have her at any cost.

Returning home, he again sought the king and bespoke his aid in securing possession of the girl. The king sent for the girl's uncle and commanded him to bring the girl home, as she had been promised Kufi for his wife. Bremba, Panah's uncle, went to the school and demanded that she be given up, saying that, as both her parents were dead, he was her rightful guardian. Panah acknowledged that he was her uncle, and the missionary surrendered her. The poor girl was carried back into heathenism much against her will, to be given to a man whom she detested; but her will was as that of a fly in a spider's web.

Thus the small, flickering spark, ignited by the torchlight of Christianity, was extinguished by the damp, foul air of paganism. Panah, whose little life seemed so promising in the mission, became as the wilted bud that fades and dies on the diseased rose bush. She was only one of the many wives of a heathen warrior, so that the tiny seed sown by the hand of the faithful missionary in the hope of a fruitful harvest perished amid the rank and poisonous weeds of African heathenism.

Perished, did I say? Never! Truthfully Carlyle said: "Beautiful it is to see and understand that no worth known or unknown can die even in this earth. The work an unknown good man had done is like a vein of water flowing hidden underground, secretly making the ground green; it flows and flows, it joins itself with other veins and veinlets, and one day it will start forth a visible perennial well."

The good already done in the transformation of little Panah may not be lost, but may, like the quiet subterranean stream, some day burst forth a living well.

THE REJECTED STONE.

"Teacher, this is the first printed copy of the selection of native hymns, just issued from our press."

The speaker was a tall, manly fellow about eighteen years old, with the broad tribal mark upon his forehead. He was smiling as if greatly pleased with the little book in his hand.

For quite a while we had been spending our evenings together trying to translate English hymns into the Kroo dialect. It was rather an arduous task, and the poverty of words in the native tongue made it a difficult one. However, we had finally succeeded, and with his own hand Twaah had set up the type, and at last it was finished.

Twelve years ago a native man came to our door, leading a scantily clad boy by the hand.

FOLK-LORE FROM AFRICA

He said: "Daddy, I come to bring you this boy. He is my own child, but I don't want him to be all the same as me. I be Krooman; I no saby God; I no saby book; but all the same I want this boy to be God man, and saby God palaver."

"Daddy," I said, "I can not take the child, for we have more children now than we can comfortably take care of. We have not plenty rice to eat, nor a mat for him to sleep on. It is not convenient to take him now."

The old man hung his head, and then said, "Let him do without rice and eat what he can find" (meaning such fruit or roots as he might find, and the little fish he might catch in the nearby stream); "and as for a place for him to sleep, let him sleep here under this shed; it will not hurt him."

But I said, "No, daddy, I am unwilling to take your boy unless he can be treated just the same as the others." The old man continued to beg for the lad, but I remained firm.

After sitting around for half a day he returned to the native town near by for the night, but before the ringing of the rising bell next morning he was back again, and came thus day after day for a week, begging that we take the boy.

We finally yielded to the man's earnest entreaties and consented to take Twaah on trial, providing we could get any help for him.

Well, the way this little Bushman took hold

of things was simply marvelous. He showed unmistakable signs of a bright mind, and in a few weeks he was able to assist others, who were there long before he was. Soon he began to pick up English words, and when we gave him a book his joy was unbounded.

His father never came back to see about him, although from time to time he sent quantities of rice, dried fish, palm oil, and pepper. We concluded he feared we might ask him to take the child away if he came, but we had grown very fond of our little Krooman and were glad we did not have to part with him.

Years passed on until Twaah was sixteen, when one day he said, "Teacher, I would like to talk with you about something."

"Well," said I, "you may come in this evening, when the prayer-hour is over." We always encourage our boys and girls to come to us whenever they have any matter that perplexes them, either about temporal or spiritual things.

Twaah came according to appointment. When we were seated he said: "I have not seen my people for many years. I would not know my mother if I should meet her, and I have come to ask your advice and your permission to visit them during our vacation."

I at once gave my consent to this request, for I thought the visit would not only benefit him, but

FOLK-LORE FROM AFRICA

his people also; for this dear boy was a strong believer in the Lord Jesus and had given himself to Him four years previously. He was an ardent worker in our little Church and Sabbath-school, besides going to other towns, taking the gospel where there was no missionary.

We made preparations for his going, and as soon as the school session was over and the work adjusted, he left for his home on the Kroo coast, more than two hundred miles away. When he reached there and made himself known, his people were delighted to see him; and although he was such a big boy, his heathen mother, much to his embarrassment, took him upon her back and walked through the town, exclaiming with joy that Twaah was still her baby boy and had returned to her again.

On the Sabbath day he gathered the people around him, and began preaching and teaching them out of God's Word. Many came to hear him as he stood preaching in the street. Some came out of curiosity, being drawn by the boy whom they had known from childhood. They gazed upon him in wonder and admiration. His words fell like seed in good soil and sprang up to the honor and glory of God.

When Twaah returned, after three months' sojourn among his people, two men came with him to ask that a teacher be sent to point them "God way," as they expressed it. They said they wanted the light, but could not find it without help.

Their earnestness was pathetic. We had no regular missionary who could go to them, therefore one of our native helpers was sent by the bishop. He was well received by the believers; but there were others, who did not believe, and they began persecuting the Christians and their leader. They beat them and disturbed their services, shaved the heads of many of the women, and rubbed cayenne pepper on their cleanly-shaven scalps.

But the more the Christians were persecuted the more earnestly they prayed and the more they increased in numbers. The result has been that many have laid down their charms and fetiches and have accepted the Savior.

Persecutions have ceased now, and we need workers to go there and teach the people and help them along in the Christ-life. We need a church for them to worship in. They are growing steadily in numbers and in faithful devotion to their newly-found Lord; but they are "babes" in Christ and must be fed.

Twaah would remain among them as their teacher, but he is anxious to prepare himself thoroughly for his life work, and so diligently applies himself to study, hoping soon to return among his people to pass on to them what he has received from others.

FOLK-LORE FROM AFRICA

OUT OF HEATHENISM

FIERCELY the tropical sun beat upon a solitary traveler who, weary and footsore, was trudging along a narrow path through the dense African "bush." He had lost his way and become separated from his carriers, and by his endeavors to retrace his steps only became more and more entangled. At last he uttered a despairing cry and called loudly the name of his head carrier.

To his utter astonishment, for he believed himself hopelessly lost, he heard a voice in response. Looking around, he espied a native boy coming toward him. The boy appeared to be about ten or twelve years of age, and wore nothing upon his body save a loin cloth. He carried an empty basket upon his head, and sauntered along with the air of one perfectly familiar with his surroundings.

"Come here, boy," said the traveler, as the boy advanced toward him. In the broken English he had picked up visiting the mission at Yallahtown, several miles distant, the lad greeted the stranger.

"Be you big daddy come from de ship?" said the boy.

"I am lost," said the gentleman. "I want to go to the mission at Yallahtown."

"It be too long way, and I done walk plenty," said the boy. "I take you wid me, daddy."

Anything seemed preferable to remaining where

he was, so the man followed the boy, who led him to his native town, not far distant, the inmates of which gave the stranger a kind welcome, and the boy's father conducted him at once to his own hut; he ordered food to be prepared, and did everything in his power to make his visitor comfortable. The natives stood eying him curiously, but withal kindly, as Dakinah—for that was the lad's name—explained to them that he had lost his way and was going to the mission.

"Be you live to come long way?" asked Dakinah's father.

"I come from the coast, and I want to reach the mission station at Yallahtown," was the answer.

"You no live git dah, for dark ketch you; it be too long way," said the native man, kindly. "To-night you sleep wid me, and to-morrow we go together to dem place."

Thus urged, the man, whose name was Mr. Wesley, remained until the next day. He felt especially drawn toward his little preserver and very grateful to him, and so persuaded the boy's father to let him place him in the mission school, after much palaver.

After placing him in the school, Mr. Wesley departed again for the coast to superintend the landing of a cargo of modern farming implements which had been sent from America, he having come to make scientific experiments in agriculture in the interest of a company seeking to develop the commercial interests of Africa.

Five years elapsed, and then he returned to the United States, taking Dakinah, who had now grown into a large, strong lad, with him, and the boy then assumed the name of his friend and patron, and was called Dakinah Wesley. Mr. Wesley placed him in an industrial school, so that he might learn to become a skilled mechanic, and Dakinah studied hard and worked diligently, showing himself an apt and ready pupil. But he had not been at the school long before he suffered the loss of his dear foster father, who died suddenly of pneumonia.

The poor lad was almost prostrated by the blow, throwing him so suddenly upon his own resources, a comparative stranger in a strange land. But controlling his grief, he began to look about for a livelihood. Mr. Allen, a friend of Mr. Wesley's and a farmer, offered him a home if he would make himself useful, which Dakinah gladly accepted, and promised to render him all the assistance in his power. He accordingly left school and went with his new friend to his home in the northwestern part of the United States.

Dakinah found this home comfortable, but he sorely missed the kindly care of his former friend. He could no longer attend school, for Mr. Allen, himself an assiduous worker, needed his help upon the farm, and Dakinah worked both late and early with such vim and energy that he soon won the confidence of his employer.

One day, as they were cutting trees preparatory to clearing land near the house, Mr. Allen observed with much pleasure how steadily Dakinah worked at his laborious task, and how the well-directed blows of his ax sent the chips flying in every direction.

"You use your ax well, my boy," remarked Mr. Allen.

"I do my best," answered Dakinah, "to make every stroke tell."

"Do you always do your best?" asked Mr. Allen, studying the boy with fresh interest.

"To do my best is always my chief desire. Mr. Wesley told me when he put me at the industrial school to study hard, and always do my best in everything, and I promised him I would, for I wanted to learn all I could, so I could go back some day and help my people."

"Do you still want to go back?" asked Mr. Allen.

"Yes, indeed, sir; it is my cherished aim, and if Mr. Wesley had lived I should have soon been ready to return to my home to help my people."

The conversation stopped here, and both resumed their work; but Dakinah had made a deep impression upon Mr. Allen by his earnestness and unselfishness, and he decided that such a boy was worthy of assistance. He felt, however, that the boy was too sensitive to accept pecuniary aid, and besides he himself did not favor such charity.

A few days afterward Mr. Allen proposed to Dakinah that he run the farm on shares, giving Kakinah one-third of the profits and he retaining two-thirds; and as Dakinah had some experience with tools, he proposed to pay him for all repairing he might do about the place. Dakinah gladly accepted the proposal, for he felt that now he would have a chance to earn something toward carrying out his long-cherished plan.

When the agreement between the two went into effect, Dakinah felt quite elated that he was now earning something for himself and was not dependent upon Mr. Allen. He applied himself diligently, and Mr. Allen had no cause to regret taking him into partnership. Thus a year passed away, and both agreed that its labor was very satisfactory, and the same bargain was made between the two for the ensuing twelvemonth.

At the end of three years Dakinah found himself able to return to school, which Mr. Allen urged him to do, for he was thoroughly imbued with a desire to help the boy, now grown to a stalwart young man, secure the training he so much wished for in order that he might return to his native land

and assist his people. Dakinah accordingly went back, and at the end of three years finished his course and graduated.

Soon afterward he received an appointment as superintendent of an industrial mission near his old home, and then his cup of joy was running over, for he had obtained the desire of his heart. During the years he was absent very little change had taken place at his home, where, it being some distance from the coast, civilization had not made much advancement among his people. The only change perceptible was one for the worse: the natives had fallen under the influence of the curse of rum, which threatens to sink Africa lower and lower into the depths of degradation and misery. The traders had penetrated far enough to introduce this article of their merchandise among the natives, and its demoralizing influence was fast working havoc among them.

Dakinah set to work with a will, and before long had his school organized and in good working shape. Being familiar with the people, he was able to make considerable advancement among them in a very short time. He filled the school with native lads, whom he taught to make little household furnishings; he taught them carpentry, brickmaking, farming, etc., how to read and write, and many other useful things. He sought out the chief men in the tribe and succeeded in getting

FOLK-LORE FROM AFRICA

their assistance and co-operation in his fight against the rum traffic. Little by little the influence of Dakinah and his helpers began to be felt; the town assumed a much more thriving appearance, the heaps of rum bottles began to disappear, and the farms received more attention.

The first visible fruit of his labor was a wooden structure built in the center of the town, for religious worship by the students of the school. Here on the Sabbath, and week days as well, Dakinah taught them the higher way of living and respect for their women. Slowly but surely Christianity, with its civilizing influence, worked a great change among this tribe.

Other workers joined Dakinah in his labor of love, and his heroic spirit and untiring zeal so influenced them that they, too, became thoroughly imbued with the love of their work; and through the combined efforts of Dakinah and his helpers the field of labor was enlarged, other additions were made to the work and a flourishing Church established. The ju-jus, witch doctors, and heathen customs disappeared entirely from the community; girls were no longer bought and sold as wives; the women were elevated, and respected and treated as equals; thrift and tidiness, temperance and civilization were everywhere apparent, and the whole tribe literally became transformed. Soon this influence spread far and wide, and other tribes and towns were uplifted and redeemed.

Dakinah was loved and revered by the people, not simply because he was one of them, but because he made them feel that he was their friend and desired to help them. He lived to see many good results of his labors, not only among his own tribe, but also among surrounding tribes. When he went to his final reward the good words he wrought were a perpetual monument to his memory.

Thus were demonstrated the possibilities of a single human life when lifted out of the darkness of heathenism and degradation and equipped with the accouterments of civilization and Christianity. Millions in Africa's wilds, like Dakinah, only wait for the uplifting power of some helpful influence to enkindle hope and lead to higher destiny.

AN AFRICAN PRODUCT.

Africa's material possibilities are wonderful; they are even marvelous. The largest gold deposits in the world are found in Africa. In the Kimberly mines the value of the diamonds taken from this single little district, a few miles square, reached a sum in excess of $400,000,000 in less than twenty years. Cecil Rhodes, Alfred Beit, Barney Barnato, F. S. P. Stow, and Paul Kruger

FOLK-LORE FROM AFRICA

obtained their enormous wealth in Africa. Liberia, which is small in comparison with the other countries of Africa, has contributed not a little to the fortune of Europeans and her own citizens. A. Woerman, of the Woerman Steamship Company, Hamburg, laid the foundation of his now large treasures in Liberia years ago. The great commercial and political interest taken in Africa by the Powers of Europe is chiefly because of its material value.

But Africa contains vastly more than material wealth. She has to give to the world more than gold and diamonds and other precious, inanimate substances. These are perishable and, while offering large and powerful attractions to ambitious individuals and imperial nations to swell their coffers, are but paltry in comparison with the greater and grander possibilities which have been, and are, constantly revealing themselves in the mental and moral uplift of Africans, as individuals of the race are given opportunity for Christian learning and are brought in contact with the benign influences of the gospel of Jesus Christ.

Nothing equals an immortal soul. "What is a man profited if he gains the whole world and lose his own soul?" or, "What will a man give in exchange for his soul?" are Scriptural queries that put tremendous emphasis upon the value of man. And when that soul is lifted from degradation,

MISSIONARY STORY SKETCHES

who can estimate its worth or measure its possibilities? An African lifted out of the darkness of heathenism into the light of civilization may not in itself as an act become a serious factor in the commercial or political life of the continent; yet who can forecast or calculate the influence of such a moral transformation in the life of a race or people?

Man is the noblest work of God and is therefore greater than material things, whatever may be the value put upon them. The untutored savage, although a pagan, is for all that superior to the lifeless metal and senseless stones that lie buried in the bowels of the earth, because man was made in the image of God and is heir to immortal life.

Our African product of this sketch is a young man of the Bassa tribe, whose history is full of interest, and whose life is not without suggestive points which bespeak the possibilities of the African. Born of heathen parentage and reared in a little native town in the interior of Liberia, he inherited all the superstitions of his tribe and locality. His home was a thatched hut built of bamboo and daubed with mud. The simplest, crudest dwelling it was.

Like all African boys, he played in the warm, bright sunshine and found keen delight in the varied sports and pastimes of his native heath.

FOLK-LORE FROM AFRICA

Clothing he had none save the insufficient and soiled rag dangling about his loins, and even this scant attire was more off than on as he played with his fellows in the quiet, meandering streams or naïvely scampered through the interlaced vines and luxuriant growth of his forest home.

The Gri-Gri Bush and Devil Bush swayed a mighty and far-reaching influence in the life of his community, and well does he recall the terrible impressions these ancient institutions made upon his childish mind in those earlier days, when their influence brooked no restraint from civilized law. Then, as now in the heart of Liberia, devil worship with all its weird and uncanny vagaries and mysteries was the all-persuasive law of the African universe. Evil spirits filled the earth and air and sky, and frequented every nook and corner of the jungles. They inhabited dark and deep caves and recesses, and brooded over and about great rocks and gigantic trees and uninviting streams. They were in majestic supremacy and were accounted worthy to receive honor and homage of their simple and deluded worshipers; even sacrificial offerings of food and drink were not despised.

It was a fundamental law of African existence, if life would be bearable and successful, charms and fetiches must be purchased of the "devil doctors" (high priests of the evil spirits), and these worn upon the body to ward off disease and guard against misfortune by propitiating these demon specters, otherwise disastrous consequences would ensue, seriously involving individuals and tribes. In the midst of such surroundings and upon such scenes our lad gazed with youthful amazement. He had no other aspiration than that which comes to the average "bush" boy, of growing up in this savage state and becoming a pronounced heathen with all the weaknesses of untrained and unenlightened humanity. Perhaps his ambition was to be a powerful native chief, rich in wives, children, cattle, and land, or a formidable warrior or daring hunter.

But this was not to be. The whole course of his life is changed. A kindly Providence directed better and larger things for this simple child of nature.

Waggie Zene, the boy's father, although a heathen and chief of his tribe, had secret longings for a better day for his people, and it was his one great desire to place his little boy, the only son of his favorite and head wife, in the Monrovia Methodist Mission, down on the beach.

On reaching Monrovia he went directly to the missionary, whose interest and love for the natives was well known, her name having been carried far into the interior. Addressing her in the best English he could command—the boy trembling in the meanwhile with fear and holding tightly to his

FOLK-LORE FROM AFRICA

father's hand as the missionary approached, as this was the lad's first time out of the native town—Waggie Zene spoke in labored, faltering inflections:

"Mammy—news ketch—we town—you be 'God woman'—you—like country people—you—teach country man pickaninny book. Dat ting—he be good for true. We—thank you—plenty, mammy. Bassa man—long time he be fool too much—dis time—he no be big fool like tudder time—he all same—Kroo man and Vey man now. He—learn book—dis time. I bring—you—dis pickaninny. He—be my boy first time—now—he—be—your boy—dis time. I be Bassa man—I—no—saby—book. Dis boy—spose he saby book, he pass me too much far and ketch Merican. I—give—you—dis—boy—mammy. Teach him—plenty—book, so—he head be—big wid Merican sense. Bomby—den he be—big man for—we—country. Den—he no lib do all dem same ting we do in we country. Den—he be we teacher and chief. We—country be fine too much proper all same Merican country."

This speech, though in broken and struggling English, was not without force, as Waggie Zene suited his inflection and gestures to his thoughts and words. It made a deep and favorable impression on the missionary; furthermore, the silent language of the boy's winsomeness and his bright and kindly eyes added strength to his father's plea in his behalf. Such a lad made a good accession to the school. On receiving a favorable reply, Waggie Zene thanked the missionary in his own native way, and, to show his thanks more tangibly, reached down and took a white chicken out of his bamboo basket, and also measuring a kru* of rice, handed these to the missionary. The gift was an expression of appreciation of the good woman's kindness, and likewise a sort of advanced installment payment for the child's education. Then, seeking to loosen the boy's tight grasp on his hand, he gently pushed him towards the outstretched hands of the missionary, who, receiving and caressing him, said to Waggie Zene, "All right, I will take good care of Dawah"—that was the boy's name—"and do my best in training him."

"Come, my child, I will not hurt you," said the missionary, speaking in the Bassa language, and with a tone that revealed tenderness and love. Dawah, yielding to her entreaties, fell into her lap, covering his face with the ample folds of her dress.

Waggie Zene, seeing an opportunity to withdraw from the room while Dawah's back was to him, slipped out and was soon down to the waterside in his little canoe, which skimmed the water under his regular and vigorous paddling like a

---

*Kru, an African measure equivalent to half a bushel.

thing of real life. The sight of Cape Mesurado and Monrovia with its cluster of houses and prominent buildings soon disappeared as he made the many bends and turns of the river. The tide was in his favor, and his little boat bore him on the placid stream as though propelled by steam or electricity. Soon he reached home, and the news of Dawah's living with the missionary spread far and wide among the surrounding tribes.

Dawah, when he turned and looked around the room and failed to see his father, began to cry bitterly and furiously. Nor would he be consoled.

"Dardar! Dardar!" he called, piteously, the large tears welling up in his bright eyes and streaming down his cheeks. Hearing no response, he nervously looked about him, brushed away the tears with his hand, and rushed wildly for the open door, determined to find his father. He would have run away but for the alertness and agility of one of the larger boys of the mission, who caught him and brought him back, his lithe uncovered body vehemently wriggling in all sorts of shapes and angles as he tried to escape, in the assertion of his savage nature. But this was not for long; the sight of a large ripe banana and mango plum had a soothing effect upon the boy as they were handed him by the teacher. They were eaten in childish haste and heartiness, and soon the tears and sobs were no more, and Dawah was fast asleep

MISSIONARY STORY SKETCHES

on the mat by the side of his new friend, whom he soon learned to love and call "teacher."

Dawah was like a fragrant flower that budded and blossomed in the sunshine and showers of his tropical clime. It was delightful to watch his gradual unfolding. He grew rapidly, and his new home, like his native heath, was congenial to him. In a few years he became a large boy, and his mental and moral growth was as perceptible as was his physical.

He remained in the mission six years and received instruction in the common English branches, together with religious and industrial training of the home. This molded his life anew and awakened dormant energies and impulses for larger preparations and usefulness. Contact in such a home furnishes many opportunities and lessons not found in text-books, and this boy's mind was alert and eager to receive impressions in this new life and situation. His teacher was well pleased with his progress in his books, and he won many a prize for proficiency in study and for his remarkable memory in committing long and involved paragraphs of Scripture and hymns. He liked to work, and when anything important had to be done requiring special care, Dawah was always the one to do it. He was thoughtful, faithful, and reliable. He enjoyed play with a keen relish, and his merry laughter and innocent fun always brought added pleasure to the home and class-room. He was a favorite with his associates.

"Dawah!" called his teacher one day, as he threw down a heavy load of wood in the yard, which fell to the ground with a loud noise. He had cut it in the woods two and one-half miles away, and this was his sixth load for the day.

Noticing it, his teacher said, earnestly, "My boy, you must not carry such heavy loads; they will injure you."

"But I am well and strong, teacher," he quickly replied, "and I don't mind it."

"That may be, my boy; but there is no necessity at all for that. I must see that each boy has a just division of the work, so that you will not be imposed upon. Such heavy bundles will flatten your head and dwarf your body. I want you to have your full strength in body as well as in mind."

"Thank you, teacher; I will always remember what you say."

Placing her hands gently upon his head, and speaking in tones of love and tenderness, she said, "What I called you for, Dawah, is to talk with you about some plans I have for you."

"What are they, teacher?"

"Well," speaking slowly and thoughtfully, "I am thinking that I ought to send you to America, that you may continue your education there, under the best possible conditions, and afterwards take the medical course. Doctors," she continued, "are so much needed in Liberia. The mortality here is so great, not so much because of the climate, but because there are so few physicians, no hospitals, and so great a lack of wisdom respecting the laws of health, hygiene, and sanitation. There is a great work for the skilled physician. No class of professional men are in more demand than they. What do you think of this, Dawah?"

"O, teacher!" he exclaimed. "You are right; that is what is needed! O, send me to America, and I promise you that I will do my best to come up to your expectation." The eloquence of action was added to Dawah's words, as he jumped around the room, thoroughly carried away with the thought.

The missionary's plans carried, and in due time Dawah, now a young man, embarked for the United States to extend his studies so as to be prepared for the medical profession. He entered Walden University, and after several years of hard study finished the academic course and passed the entrance examination for his entrance in Meharry Medical College. In due course he graduated from the institution, standing as high as scores of others born under superior advantages. While pursuing his studies he honorably supported himself, and thus maintained his manhood.

He returned to Africa after an absence of

FOLK-LORE FROM AFRICA

eleven years, and entered upon the work of his noble profession.

Such examples bespeak promise and hope for Africa, and likewise furnish convincing argument in favor of Christian missions.

What an inviting sphere of activity, and what a pleasing future lies before him!

The practice of medicine in Africa, where stubborn diseases have reaped such awful harvest through the long, long centuries, and where sanitary measures have scarcely begun to operate, is a Godsend. Africa needs no messengers more urgently than Christian physicians, who in the practice of the healing art perform a service of unspeakable value to mankind.

The services of Dr. S. M. E. Goheen, a medical missionary of the Liberia Mission in 1836, were of incalculable value in those days when disease and death made frightful inroads among colonists and missionaries. His name stands high among the immortals of that consecrated band of men and women of that early period who served the cause of foreign missions and who labored for Africa's redemption.

Our African product, therefore, in line with the professional labors of the beloved and sainted Goheen, has a noble work, a great work, and, with his tribal identity and intimate knowledge of aboriginal customs and dialects, is well prepared to render Liberia and Methodism great and valuable service. May he possess all the qualities of brain, heart, and life that shall make him a skillful and successful physician and a perennial blessing to suffering humanity in Africa.

"All that a man hath will he give for his life," is a maxim of universal application. The physician, therefore, who provides the remedies to guard, preserve, and support life, and to battle with stubborn disease, is a benefactor to mankind and richly deserves the lasting gratitude of his fellows.

It is a source of encouragement to know that our product has the increasing respect and love of his compatriots, and his reputation as a skillful physician is growing with the years. May his record ever be worthy and his service such as shall immortalize his name!

GETTING SAVED

At the daily prayer services we had been talking to our people concerning the need of personal acceptance of Christ. They had been under religious instruction, and many of them were trying to live according to the New Testament standard.

One night we had for our lesson the story of Nicodemus and the new birth. They were very

FOLK-LORE FROM AFRICA

much interested, and every one who had not already experienced what it is to be "born again" was anxious to come into this close relation with Christ.

After the meeting, which was of unusual warmth on this particular night, one of the boys, Twado, came up and earnestly said that he wanted to know more about Jesus. In his eyes was every sign of anxiety and heart-longing.

We retired to a small room to talk the matter over, and to sing and pray. For an hour we read together from St. John's Gospel, and I talked and explained the Word to him. Then we knelt down to pray, with the open Bible before us.

No sooner were we on our knees than Twado seemed to lose all thought of my presence and began calling mightily to God to save him from his sins. He threw himself upon the floor and cried aloud for pardon, praying in both English and in his native tongue. There he lay wrestling in agony for some little time, when his pleadings were suddenly changed into shouts of joy and gladness, as he cried: "I am saved! I am saved!"

Then, with beaming face and clapping hands, he sang:

> " I am so wondrously saved from sin ;
> Jesus so sweetly abides within.
> There at the cross, where He took me in,
>   Glory to His name !"

MISSIONARY STORY SKETCHES

Twado's face was illuminated and beautiful. Eagerly he seized my hand, saying: "I have found Jesus, and He is my Savior. He is precious to me."

This was the beginning of a revival of religion. Before the meetings closed every one on the station was rejoicing in Jesus' love. The fire began to burn elsewhere, and soon other stations were ablaze with religious fervor. Conviction was abroad among the people, and there were many contrite ones who flocked to the altar by scores yearning for salvation. Weeping penitents were everywhere—in the churches, homes, streets, and highways—seeking the Lord. Natives from the heathen towns, with downcast countenances, were seen along the paths and in the groves under deep conviction of sin imploring God for forgiveness. Without restraint or disguise they gave vent to their feelings, weeping and praying aloud wherever they were.

The following incident has been told by one of the missionaries, showing how the natives were affected in a similar revival some years previous to this:

"In the highest state of the excitement, after the burial of our little boy I was out at the graveyard superintending the clearing away of the weeds and improving the missionaries' burying-ground. Large numbers of the natives were under deep conviction. Some of them had not partaken of food for several days. They were solemnly pacing through the grounds or lying prostrate full length on the graves, on the damp earth, under a sun almost vertical, with only their heads covered with their rude cloth.

"When asked what they were doing, their answer was, 'Live, pray, find God.' Fearing their native superstition might have something to do with their praying in the burial ground and lying on the graves, they were advised to abandon these places and told they could find the Lord at home or otherwise. They at once ceased this objectionable feature in their conduct. Many of them were converted. They gave very clear accounts of their conversion, relying in the blood of the Crucified."

Like the revival described by the missionary, this one also made a profound impression on the natives, and hundreds were brought into the fold of Christ. The Churches witnessed unusual times of refreshing from the presence of the Lord; the people were quickened in the faith and spiritual life; the spirit of grace and supplication was copiously poured out upon the people.

Not only are there instances of sudden outbreaks of religious enthusiasm such as this on the field, but salvation has come in quiet ways under the influence of the preached Word and other means of grace.

MISSIONARY STORY SKETCHES

There is the case of a young man in one of our towns who rather scoffed at the idea of religion. He would not listen to the gospel, nor would he come into our meetings. It seemed to be a delight to him to stride by the open door of the church while the people were engaged in worship. One Sabbath morning, however, when the rain came down in torrents, this young man was seen in the audience among the faithful few who had braved the storm on that day. His demeanor was quiet and reverential, despite his skepticism regarding Christianity. His presence in church was surprising, the more so on such a day.

I afterwards learned that his motive was to hear the new missionary, who had recently arrived in the country. Well, the service opened; the Holy Spirit was present, and His presence was deeply felt in all hearts. The missionary spoke with great liberty; his theme, "Contrary Winds," and his text the words found in St. Mark's Gospel: "And He saw them toiling and rowing; for the wind was contrary unto them; and about the fourth watch of the night He cometh unto them, walking upon the sea, and would have passed by them."

The preacher talked about the storm on the Sea of Galilee, where the disciples were toiling and rowing, and how Jesus came to them in their extremity, calming the fury of the winds and rescuing the despairing ones. Then the application of the lesson was made, producing a deep impression upon all. The young man listened attentively to the discourse. He felt that the sermon was a direct message to him, for like the storm-tossed disciples of old, he was beset by contrary winds, and his weary soul longed for some safe anchorage from the surging billows and a Divine Pilot to conduct him there.

The service over, he went quietly and quickly away to hide the deep emotion caused by the sermon. Several days later he came around to the mission house and asked for the missionary, to whom he said: "My dear sir, I have had no peace of mind since I heard your discourse a few days ago on 'Contrary Winds.' That represents my condition exactly. I am tossed about, and I want peace. Tell me how to find it."

The missionary prayed and talked to him, trying to lead him into the light. The young man went away somewhat helped, but yet having a heavy heart. His purpose, however, was fixed: he was determined to find Christ.

Three days later he again returned to the missionary with a happy heart, saying that he had at last found Jesus and that great peace flooded his soul. His conversion was a town topic. It had a salutary effect upon his worldly associates, who, like him, sought and found salvation. And there was great joy in that city.

MISSIONARY STORY SKETCHES

In Beaboo, one of the interior towns, there was a native young man who had an attack of rheumatism. His people insisted upon his going to the "devil doctor" for treatment. The young man hesitated, but was finally persuaded by his heathen relatives. This is his own story:

"They put me in the 'devil doctor's' hands for treatment. I was not allowed to bathe, nor to have my hair cut. We made many sacrifices of dogs and fowls to the 'devil doctor.' All of the bones were kept, and these I was compelled to wear around my neck. The 'devil doctor' made medicine for me and gave me many fetiches to wear upon my body. I did not get better under such treatment. One night I dreamed that the thing I was doing was not right, and I made up my mind to leave there and go to the mission station that I heard of. I told the 'devil doctor' that I was better and I was going home. He was quite willing for me to go, for he knew that I was not better, and he thought that I would soon return, bringing larger dashes and money from my people. He gave me plenty of medicine and several more fetiches; told me not to eat rice from my own farm, nor to allow fish to be brought in my house. I went home, but continued to grow worse.

"The dream repeated itself, and I called my wife and told her I was going to the mission house to see if they could do anything for me. When

FOLK-LORE FROM AFRICA

I reached the mission I took off my charms and gave them to my father and told him to burn them. I knew they were false, and I wanted the truth. I had not only come to the mission because I was sick, but also because I wanted to do 'God way' and leave heathen way behind. I went into the service, it being Sunday, and noticed the interpreter did not 'pass the word' correctly. He was afraid to tell the people just what the missionary was saying, and he told them what pleased him. This greatly troubled me, and when I had a chance I told them just what was said. They did not like me and said I would break down the country. So they began to persecute me. I was beaten, and they took my child from me. I prayed to God, and got my child back again and put it in the mission also. Now we are all happy, for I am not only cured in body, but in soul also. I have found the true light. My wife and child both rejoice in the light that has come to us. We have sworn to break off from heathen life and serve the Lord."

The conversion of old King Hodge, one of the most influential kings on the Liberian coast, was an interesting one, and perhaps one of the most valuable to the cause of missions.

King Hodge was king of the Gidebo or Grebo people, who lived at Big Town. This is a large, native town near Harper, Cape Palmas.

MISSIONARY STORY SKETCHES

One day one of our missionaries went over to Big Town to talk to the natives there. King Hodge heard what was said, and it greatly pleased and interested him. He asked the missionary to come back and tell him more about the "God palaver." This he did, and King Hodge was converted, becoming a strong advocate for the spread of the gospel among his tribe. He afterwards became a preacher and spoke with great power.

This was the beginning of a prosperous work among the natives of Big Town. They built for themselves a thatch church, which was soon too small, when another and more substantial one was erected and crowds of his people joined. It was during this time that the use of sasswood was discontinued among this branch of the Gedebo people. Other crude and inhuman practices were also discontinued.

Polygamy is practiced among the Gedebo people, as is customary among all African tribes; but, following the example of King Hodge, many denounced polygamy and embraced the Christian system of marriage, meekly seeking to live according to the teachings of Christ and the apostles.

Years afterwards, when the old king was dying, he sent for the missionary and caused his will to be written, in which he bequeathed his children and tribe to the Church of his choice. Thus his tribe and family were placed within the bosom of the Church.

FOLK-LORE FROM AFRICA

Many of his girls and boys were put in the mission homes and schools, and have since developed into strength and usefulness to the Church and country.

The most encouraging feature of missionary work in Africa is the conversion of the untutored savage, his transformation from moral night to the marvelous light of the gospel of Christ. This work—seeking first the kingdom and righteousness, is paramount.

The African is a splendid subject for evangelism. His simple, childlike faith, his docility, and sympathetic heart, like the fertile soil of his native heath, is virgin ground for gospel seed. He is not an atheist, nor has he the ancient and effete civilization of Asiatic countries. He is intensely religious, and his religion is as much a part of himself as his arm or leg. To him the universe is controlled by spirit, and his creed is to be in peaceful harmony with the great world of spirits.

While his religious instincts seem out of harmony with Christian principles and often find expression in brutal practices, nevertheless his abiding faith in a higher power to direct and control the affairs of men, if properly cultivated and directed, will eventually lead him to accept the whole truth of Christ.

Like mankind everywhere, he deeply needs salvation through Jesus Christ. When Christ is presented and exalted before him, he is wondrously drawn to Him. The silent power of our holy religion, in precept and practice, is the only and true remedy for Africa. There is no other.

CLASPING HANDS WITH AFRICA

"The spirit of Melville B. Cox, our first missionary to Africa, yet lives, and his immortal words, 'Let a thousand fall before Africa be given up,' I fancy I hear again," was the remark of an elderly lady as she congratulated the speaker who had made the principal address of the evening in connection with the anniversary services of the Missionary Society held at the annual session of one of our Southern Conferences.

She passed down the aisle of the church leaning on the arm of a friend, for she required support in walking. She was not as strong as in former years; old age, with its attendant disabilities, was approaching. But her heart was as young as ever, and her enthusiasm for foreign missions was as great as when she first responded to the call, many years ago, and laid herself upon God's altar.

At the door of the church had gathered a group of young men and women, earnestly discussing the address to which they had intently

FOLK-LORE FROM AFRICA

listened. The message evidently had made a profound impression upon these members of the Epworth League branch of their local Church, who constituted the special committee on missions, having "Africa" as the topic for discussion; and the character of the study for the month was such as required information that could best be given by one having large acquaintance with the field and knowing its essential needs. Now they were very anxious to know more about Africa, the least known of the great fields of the Church, and particularly Liberia, the oldest of our foreign missions.

The remark of the lady touching Melville B. Cox, whose name is a household word throughout Methodism and whose ringing watchword never ceases to inspire, at once made her an object of attention. What she said was repeated and communicated to the group, and it soon became known that she was a retired missionary from Africa, having labored for many years in Liberia, and was the only living link connecting the early days of the Liberia mission, immediately following the death of Cox, with the present. She was temporarily residing with friends in the village.

Being introduced to the young people by the pastor, she commented at length on the address of the evening, and on learning of their plans and work in relation to Africa, warmly commended their proposed program, and in response to their urgent invitation she kindly consented to make an address on "Liberia, and Our Work There."

When bidding them good-night, she said: "Young friends, you can not imagine how happy I am to see such continued and growing interest in Africa. We can not be faithful to God and leave Africa out of our thoughts and prayers and plans. We are under bonds to the 'Dark Continent.'"

Referring particularly to Liberia, she said, with a tremor in her voice: "After twenty-five years of service there I must confirm the judgment of our first missionary, who said, after a survey of the field: 'There is not in the wide world a field that promises the sincere efforts of a Christian community, a richer harvest. There is not in the wide world a spot to which Americans owe so much to human beings as to this same degraded Africa.' May your work," she concluded, prayerfully and with deep emotion, "be blessed of the Lord and yield an abundant harvest in the years to come, to the honor and glory of His name."

The speaker's memory of details back in the early thirties was surprising. She remembered when interest in foreign missions began, and when, like a tidal wave, the missionary spirit swept over our beloved Methodism, and upon our altars the flame of love and earnest desire for Africa's redemption burned with lambent glow.

FOLK-LORE FROM AFRICA

How well she could recall the time and place and circumstance of her own conversion under the faithful ministrations of her beloved pastor, long since gone to his reward; and her full surrender to Christ, and of offering herself for the mission field; of the long and eventful years there. The scene of all this, like a panoramic view, passed vividly before her, and it seemed as if she were living again the life of other days as she reverted to the past.

She had been a prominent character in mission work in Liberia, and had been very successful. Her motto had always been "Service or sacrifice," and her life was an apt illustration of this. Although she knew from experience what it was to brave the perils and dangers of pioneer life in a heathen land, of being separated at long intervals from home and friends, and shut in, as it were, amidst the gloom and depression of pagan darkness, her own life being but a tiny light in the vitiated atmosphere of uncivilized life; yet hers were also the sweet joys and ample rewards which unselfish love and altruistic service bring to those who thus labor for Christ and humanity. And to have the privilege of bringing a glorious message direct from the field, the scene of earlier years, and witness the hearty response, the new outburst of interest, and awakening of missionary enthusiasm in that field, was a benediction to her soul, and it was with difficulty that she had restrained her feeling while the meeting was in progress.

One of the bishops of Africa, fresh from his first episcopal tour, ten years ago, made the address of the evening before the Annual Conference holding its missionary anniversary. His message revealed a comprehensive grasp of Africa, with a mastery of facts and a fund of information which was amazing. He had made a two years' study of the entire continent, reading the best books on the subject and conversing with men in all ranks and conditions: rulers of kingdoms and republics, governors, travelers, scientists, heads of commercial and industrial enterprises, paramount chiefs and humble natives. He had traveled on land and sea, in every possible mode of conveyance, from the magnificent steamers on the North Atlantic to the crude native canoes of the African rivers; in carts drawn by bullocks, hammocks swung by men; on horseback, oxback, and on foot, while touring the continent and superintending his great parish.

His episcopal office, although in the technical sense restricted, was nevertheless continental in extent and vast in possibilities. Such a field and theme quickened thought and facilitated speech. He told of the colossal schemes, commercial, political, and industrial, that European nations were

FOLK-LORE FROM AFRICA

projecting, all looking toward the development of the "Dark Continent," that has slept for ages but now is aroused from its lethargy. With a statesmanlike view encompassing a vast continent, he saw rising kingdoms of ebon tribes emerging out of darkness, and degradation into life and light, into progress and power.

His eloquence was irresistible. Continuing, he told in stirring, burning words the story of our work in Liberia, Angola, and Rhodesia. He pleaded passionately for reinforcement and a forward, aggressive movement into the interior; and laying on the hearts of the people, who hung upon his words, the burden of Africa's redemption, he closed his masterly discourse with a never-to-be-forgotten appeal that stirred every soul and melted all to tears. His hearers were led to see Africa in a new light and to recognize as never before the peculiar claims which the neglected tribes of the Dark Continent have upon Christendom.

Several of the most promising young men and women consecrated themselves to the work.

It is easy to imagine the new life enkindled in the cause of missions in this community by the bishop's address and the presence of the missionary from Africa. Every department of the Church was benefited. The Epworth League especially was alive with missionary enthusiasm. Old and

MISSIONARY STORY SKETCHES

young became interested, and all looked forward eagerly to the approaching session of the society when the field in which they were especially interested would come under review by one who had made it her life study and work.

Several weeks having passed, the date for the special service arrived. The committee to whom was submitted all the details of the meeting, spared no pains in their efforts to make the occasion all it should be in point of interest and success. When the hour arrived to begin, the magnificent and spacious hall was crowded with eager listeners, who greeted the veteran missionary with warmth of feeling and delight. The hymn of Bishop Heber, played by the organist and sung by the choir and audience, seemed never more appropriate. The lines—

"Where Africa's sunny fountains
Roll down their golden sand "—

woke response in sympathetic natures whose vibrations were not in discord with the stirring music.

The psalm which describes the coming glory of the Messiah and portrays a sublime and decisive victory over all His enemies, declaring that the heathen and the uttermost parts of the earth are Jehovah's rightful inheritance, was impressively read. A simple, earnest prayer was offered, after which came the address for the evening.

FOLK-LORE FROM AFRICA

The president of the League was brief in his remarks. In introducing the speaker he said:

"I am indeed happy to present the speaker of the evening to you: a lady who for many years was a successful missionary in Liberia. She is now honorably retired and sojourning in our village. We are most fortunate in being thus honored with one in our midst so eminent in service and so well prepared to speak on the subject of foreign missions, Africa in particular. In her we have a 'living link' not only connecting the past of that field with the present, but uniting Africa in America with Africa beyond the seas. I am sure I voice your sentiment in extending to her a hearty welcome and wishing for her yet many years to thrill the Church with her story of devoted service in our most difficult foreign field. I pray that her message to us will be blessed of God, deepening our interest in the great cause of missions and tending to the furtherance of the gospel in that land of moral and spiritual night."

Addressing the chairman and audience, and congratulating the young people of the League for their interest in foreign missions, the missionary spoke as follows:

"Africa is in the thought and heart of our great Church as never before. From the days of Cox to the present the interest has remained, and while there were times when it seemed that the

Church had almost forgotten the rallying cry and dream of her first hero of African missions, this was but a calm, not unlike the lull of the sea which precedes the rising tide.

"It is our privilege to-day to witness the dawn of what is to be a bright and glorious future. A new era has come for Africa. While the continent is yet Africa in point of identity, there has arisen in recent years a new Africa with wonderful possibilities, and with a future that brightens with the advancing years.

"This is God's hour for Africa. It means better things for the continent, the veil of mystery lifted, the dense darkness and a vast closed land opened to civilization and the gospel of Jesus Christ. The nations of Europe have parceled out the continent among themselves, and in their greed for power and increased possessions may mean chiefly the conquest of lands and the subjugation of tribes for sordid ends; but God means the redemption of Africa that has long waited in darkness and death.

"The partitioning of the continent has opened the way for the gospel. Misrule, irregularities, evils, and even atrocities as they exist to-day in the basin of the Congo and in the other parts of Africa can not long remain. Like the slave trade, they must in time all pass away. The continent is to be free from every curse and shame and its

FOLK-LORE FROM AFRICA

people lifted out of degradation into life and liberty.

"Christian missions are following in the path of exploration, commerce, trade, and political spheres of influence. They are already exerting a powerful influence in strategic centers on the coast and are gradually pushing their way through the dense, dark forests and jungles into regions beyond; transforming the continent, so that barbarism is giving place to peaceful industries, paganism to civilization, crude native huts to thriving towns and cities.

"The conquest of the cross in Uganda, in the face of opposition and bitter persecution, bespeaks promise and hope for Africa, and yet Uganda is only one of the many miracles of missions in Africa. Missionary achievements may be counted now by scores. Products of missionary labor as exhibited in such men as Samuel A. Crowther, James Johnson, King Khama, Paul, the 'Apostle of the Congo,' and King Hodge of Liberia, and others, are multiplying year by year. Soon there will be a great host of Africa's own sons and daughters enlisted under the banner of our Christ to achieve yet greater victories in His name.

"To David Livingstone perhaps more than to any other single individual are we indebted for the revelations that have come from the Dark Continent. For thirty years his life was spent in an

MISSIONARY STORY SKETCHES

unwearied effort to evangelize the native races of the continent; to explore the undiscovered secrets; to abolish the desolating slave trade of Central Africa, which he described as the 'open sore' of the world. He prayed that heaven's richest blessings would come down on every one, American, English, and Turk, who would aid in its healing and eradication.

"Livingstone was most abundant in labors under circumstances most trying. He threaded his way through the heart of Africa, penetrating the vast jungles, the dense and dangerous forests, from the western to the eastern coast. He explored a number of the great lakes and rivers and mountains of Africa, and discovered the Victoria Falls, an object of wonder and beauty. At times he was wasted by African fevers and other scourges; but nothing daunted, he continued his great work, which has immortalized his name and places the civilized world everlastingly in his debt. All honor to David Livingstone, missionary and hero of the Dark Continent!

"Africa is a great and vast continent, extending from north to south, nearly 6,000 miles in length, and at its greatest breadth 4,850. It has an area of nearly 12,000,000 square miles—a hundred times as much as England, Ireland, Scotland, and Wales combined. It is three times as large as all Europe, or four times as much as the United

FOLK-LORE FROM AFRICA

States. It contains one-fourth of all the land surface of the globe, and has a population of upwards of 200,000,000 souls.

"Circumstances, chiefly of a geographical character, have been against the development of the continent. These have given it the name of 'Pariah of Continents;' have made it for centuries a closed land. Nature, while lavishing her most bounteous gifts there, has at the same time imposed certain barriers which hamper no other continent. But when Africa's geographical problem is solved, the way will be opened for advancement by leaps and bounds.

"What a giant continent in territorial extent, and what a sublime purpose the Creator must have had in making a country with such huge proportions and limitless possibilities! Certainly the near future must witness a great and constant unfolding of that purpose as the Church, with an awakened and enlightened conscience, with apostolic faith and undiminished heroism, pushes the victories of the cross in that vast empire of darkness.

"Africa's hope is in the successful and perfect work of Christian missions. Our earnest prayer is that she may receive, as her imperative needs demand, such wise and adequate consideration of the Church as shall make possible the speedy realization of that hope.

"With this scheme of work the Methodist Episcopal Church sympathized heartily. It looked upon the movement as a providential opening for the extension of the kingdom of Christ in Africa and an open door for the heathen tribes beyond.

"Our Church was therefore among the earliest to enter Liberia, and in 1832 sent out her first missionary, Melville B. Cox. Twelve years previous Daniel Coker, a Methodist preacher, one of the eighty-eight emigrants on the ship *Elizabeth*—the *Mayflower* of Liberia—organized the company on shipboard into the Methodist Episcopal Church. The ship was ten days out from New York, and ice-bound. On Cox's arrival he found the Church Coker had planted and fostered. This proved the tiny seed from which has grown our Liberian Methodism.

"Although of feeble health, knowing that he would soon succumb to the severities of the African climate, Cox entered into the work with all the enthusiasm of youth and all the intensity of his enfeebled constitution.

"When he reached Liberia he began at once to study the field and formulate plans for the work. Seventy-five years have passed away since he presented his scheme of work to the Missionary Society, and yet his recommendations bear but few marks of antiquity. Their adaptions to present needs and conditions are surprising, and the breadth of view and grasp which they reveal seem to furnish the key to solve the problems that confront our work to-day, as well as that of missions generally in Africa.

"As to the field itself, he recognizes its importance. To him Africa furnished numerous objects for the philanthropists, and the most promising opportunity for missionary enterprise. In his broad vision he saw no somber outlook, but rather large and whitening fields of ripening grain only waiting the sickle of the faithful reaper. He was a great leader, aggressive, daring, optimistic. What he accomplished in so brief a period was marvelous. His ambition was to literally line the coast with strong stations and push with all possible energy his work interiorward as far as possible, making Liberia a 'great and effectual door' for the evangelization of the continent. To do this his plan was to occupy strategic centers, enter providential openings, master native languages, and reach surrounding tribes.

"After a lapse of seventy-five years his recommendations and plans to the Board strike me as statesmanlike and wise. Cox was inspired. Certainly he must have been under the guidance of Him whose counsels are unerring. I believe that along the line mapped out by our first missionary lieth a victory hitherto unrealized. Unquestion-

MISSIONARY STORY SKETCHES

ably it deserves sober, prayerful thought. To come fully up to Cox's idea, even to surpass it, should be the impassioned ambition of his successors in this day of enlarged opportunity and responsibility.

"It is a source of encouragement to know that the work planted by Cox has continued through a line of worthy successors for seventy-five years. They have wrought nobly and deserve the everlasting gratitude of the Church. Sometimes the results of the Liberia Mission have been compared with those of other more prosperous fields, much to the disparagement of Liberia. But results may not always be adequately estimated in figures. The rate of gain in membership, though small when compared with the outlay in money and men, and with our stronger missions in the foreign fields, is, however, by no means the only outcome of the presence and work of the Church in the republic.

"This is its least product. Its largest is of a kind that only an omniscient mind can measure and record. If it is possible to count by figures the work of the Church in that field, then it is possible to weigh and estimate the silent yet potent influences which have issued through their seventy-five years from the work and presence of the Church in Liberia.

"Methodism was contemporaneous with the in-

FOLK-LORE FROM AFRICA

fant State. It has contributed largely to the moral worth of the republic, and has been a great vitalizing force in making for righteousness and progress against the works and forces of evil and heathenism. As our oldest foreign mission it has a romantic history. Its thrilling story never ceases to charm.

"To-day the work is under the leadership of a son of Africa, Bishop Isaiah B. Scott, supported by a band of faithful workers, both of Liberia and America. Educated blacks from our schools in the Southland, children of parents who felt the galling yoke of bondage, are now helping to reclaim and redeem their less fortunate brethren from heathenism in Africa. Thus through them and others of the Church, America and Africa are *clasping hands*, and in Christian fellowship the strong are not only helping to bear the infirmities of the weak, but seeking to uplift and redeem the benighted continent.

"May there be no backward steps in this great work—no want of faith and consecration; no lack of workers, nor retrenchment of funds; but a steady marching forward to the goal of an evangelized and redeemed land and people."

Thus spoke the devoted missionary, and the vast audience listened eagerly to every word of the message from beginning to end. And is it any

MISSIONARY STORY SKETCHES

wonder that concern in foreign missions received a new birth of interest from that service? The League became ablaze with missionary enthusiasm and, as an outlet for its energies, placed itself in direct contact with the field, thus too "Clasping Hands With Africa."

II

MYTHS—LEGENDS—FOLK-LORE

NATIVE STORIES

Story-telling is the one never-failing amusement of the African. These stories are to foreigners well-nigh interminable. There is no unseemly haste in the make-up of the native. It matters not to him or his audience if he consumes three hours in telling a yarn that might be condensed into ten minutes. There is endless repetition and elaboration of every detail, all of which his listeners enjoy. In fact, a man who speaks concisely and tersely enjoys no popularity as a story-teller. Variety is not much sought after, the natives holding the idea that the old stories are good, and good things will bear repeating.

There is a close resemblance in all the traditions of the country, though of course each tribe has its own local stories, so that it is quite customary to ask a stranger who is visiting a native village to relate a stock story of his native village.

The natives have a large fund of myths, legends, and folk-lore, which they tell with good effect whenever they would illustrate some truth or make a lucid and forceful impression on their hearers. Their conversations and palavers abound

MISSIONARY STORY SKETCHES

with these quaint reminiscences and incidents, many of which show wonderful grasp and insight into human nature. The natives of Liberia are adepts in the art of story-telling, and so their social hours are enlivened and made delightful by these interesting and original recitals, which they give in their native dialects with inimitable zest and effect.

FEMBAR'S CURIOSITY

Once there was a man named Jarbar, who had come from a foreign country to marry Fembar. He settled in the new country, and one day when he was working on his farm he saw a very strange serpent; it was immense and had large and small parts alternating, and everywhere he went on the farm he met some part of that serpent.

Soon he noticed that he understood the language of all animals, reptiles, and birds—for all have their own tongue—but he was warned not to impart to any one knowledge gained in this way, but to keep inviolate the secret of everything he heard. This gift of understanding was the result of having seen the serpent.

For a long period of time Jarbar obeyed this injunction, and greatly enjoyed the novelty of hearing what all the animal kingdom had to say, for they are often very wise. But one day, as he was eating dinner with Fembar, they received news of the death of her father. The next day she put her home in order and prepared to go to her native town to join the mourners.

In the morning, when she had everything arranged and ready to start, her husband heard a bird say, "Since you are putting everything away, how about us whom you are leaving here?" and then laughed.

His wife became angry and declared that he was laughing because of her bereavement and because she was going to leave him for awhile; and though he denied it, she remained suspicious, and finally in desperation he told her that if he revealed the cause of his laughter it would result in his death. She insisted, however, and at last he told her. Alas! shortly afterwards he died for having disobeyed the command of the reptile.

This sad blow taught the wife that one should never be so curious as to insist upon knowing something which it is better for one not to know.

A WOMAN TRANSFORMED INTO A LEOPARD

A man and a woman were once journeying through the bush. The woman had her baby strapped upon her back as she walked along upon the tedious journey, which lay over a rough path overgrown with vines and shrubbery. They had nothing to eat with them, and they became very hungry while traveling along.

As they emerged from the heavily wooded forest into a grassy plain they came upon a herd of bush cows quietly grazing.

The man said to the woman, "You have the power of transforming yourself into whatever you like; change now to a leopard and capture one of the bush cows, that I may have something to eat and not perish."

The woman looked at the man significantly and said, "Do you really mean what you ask, or are you joking?"

"I mean it," said the man, for he was very hungry.

The woman untied the baby from her back and put it upon the ground. The hair began growing out upon her neck and body. She dropped her loin cloth; a change came over her face. Her hands and feet changed, and there were claws. In fact, a wild leopard was in a few moments standing before the man, staring at him with fiery eyes. The poor man was frightened nearly to death and ran to a tree for protection.

He climbed up, and, looking down, saw the poor little baby almost within the leopard's jaws. He was afraid to come down and rescue the baby. However, when the leopard saw that the man was terribly frightened and full of terror, she ran away to the flock of cattle. She captured a large young heifer, which she dragged back to the foot of the tree to the man, who was still as far up in its top as he could go. From there he cried out and begged the leopard piteously to transform herself into a woman again.

Slowly the hair receded, and a gradual change took place until the woman stood before the man again. So frightened had the poor man been that he could scarcely believe his own eyes and was afraid to come down until he saw the woman take up her cloth and tie her baby to her back again. Then she said to him, "Never ask a woman to do a man's work again."

While the women do most of the work, such as caring for the farms, raising breadstuffs, fishing, etc., yet it is considered man's work to do the hunting and bring in the meat for the family.

A MELUSINE STORY FROM THE GOLD COAST

A poor man of Chama was one day walking toward the village of Abu-anu, very sad at heart because he had lost his wife. But as he went along his way he was stopped by a woman, who noticed how cast down he was, and asked him the cause, whereupon he told her of his loss.

MISSIONARY STORY SKETCHES

And so they talked awhile together; and so attractive was the woman that before they parted he asked her to become his wife, which at first she refused to do. But afterwards she consented, and they went to his home, where he told his friends she was his wife.

After a time she wanted to see her people again, and asked her husband to permit her to go to them, which he consented to do, provided he also might go. For some reason the woman hesitated, and did not seem to wish this; but finally she consented. So they started out, and journeyed toward the sea.

On the way, as they were discussing various things, she turned to him and said, anxiously, "When you have seen my people, and we return, will you not laugh at me?" Earnestly he assured her he would not even mention her relatives, were it disagreeable to her.

When they reached the sea she told him she was a fish, her relatives were fishes, and their home, of course, was in the ocean. As she spoke the breakers splashed at their feet, and she instructed him to follow her when she dived in the third, as this would lead to her native place. So again promising her to preserve secrecy, he followed her into the breaker.

At her home they greeted her with joy and gave him a warm greeting when they learned that he was her husband, and assigned to him a house which they told him not to go out of under any circumstances. One night he saw some young fishes at play, and wanted to go out and witness their sport more clearly, but refrained because of the admonition of his wife's relatives. But three days afterward, seeing them again, he determined to go anyway. But in this there lay grave danger, as he had upon entering the ocean partaken of the nature of a fish and gave forth the phosphorescent light which fishes do at night, and not recognizing his danger went too near the surface of the water, where he was espied by some fishermen, one of whom harpooned him.

Happily for him, his relatives saw his danger and hastened to his relief. But try as they might, they could not pull him to the bottom of the sea, and so begged a passing shark to cut the rope fastened to the harpoon. The shark gladly rendered his assistance and immediately severed the rope. They then took him back to their home, and, taking out the deathly instrument, tended his wounds until he was entirely recovered.

When the day arrived on which he was to depart with his wife for their home on the land (which was as soon as he was well, as they were afraid some other evil might befall him), his wife's relatives gave him the harpoon and told him to secrete it; so when he arrived at his home he hid it under the thatched roof of the house.

And thus nothing eventful happened for seven years; but after that lapse of time the people of the house wanted to rethatch it, and the man forgot to remove the hidden harpoon, which had almost passed out of his memory. So it was discovered by the owner, who declared at once that it was his, and one which years before he had discharged at a large fish in the sea.

The man tried to keep it, but this led to his being quizzed as to how he came in possession of it, and reluctantly he had to explain the story.

A while after this another wife, whom he had married when he and his fish wife had returned from her home, quarreled with her, and in their anger they spoke of one another in hard terms, till finally the second wife called the first a fish. Being very sensitive about this, as was shown when she had asked her husband years before not to laugh at her because of her origin or her home and people, she was deeply wounded, and with hurt pride she sought her husband and told him of what had occurred, blaming him for having insisted upon going with her to her home, years before, when she did not want him to. "I am going back; I am going to leave you once and for all, for I will not live in a place where I am scorned and ridiculed, and my children also."

FOLK-LORE FROM AFRICA

Now, her husband loved her very much, and therefore he tried hard to persuade her to stay, but in vain. The woman again set off and journeyed seaward, accompanied by her pleading husband. When the shore was reached she bade her husband good-bye forever, and her two oldest children; taking her youngest with her, she dived into the sea and was gone from him for all time, leaving him bowed down with grief.

None of the descendants of the Bonito, which are very numerous in Chama, will ever eat the bonito or safur to this day.

HOW DISPOSITIONS ARE GIVEN

A traveler in a far country was shown the sights, and among other things was led into a yard where a man bearing logs of wood was dashing them in a fearful manner among men and animals, regardless of consequences. He was then shown a man of gentle, winning disposition, entirely unlike the woodman. Others of various characteristics were shown the traveler, who inquired as to the meaning of these things.

His companion, who was the lord of the place, told him that the place he was visiting was the spirit land, where men were created and the dispositions they possess on the earth among men were given them there.

MISSIONARY STORY SKETCHES

THE DIFFERENCE BETWEEN PLANT LIFE AND ANIMAL LIFE

The natives are children of nature and live out of doors most of the time, observing closely Nature's workings.

In many towns where there are barricade fences built of green saplings, one frequently sees branches bursting forth from these logs, which begin to send out green shoots and leaves. Some young men, noting this, one day asked an older man of their family the reason for it.

In reply the old man said: "When the 'Great Spirit' had made man, it was discovered that man would die. Therefore the 'Great Spirit' made a medicine to make man immortal, and sent it to him by a white fowl. But the fowl traveled so slowly that an eagle flew down and took the medicine and flew away with it.

"In the swiftness of his flight he did not notice that he was spreading it broadcast through the forest, on the trees and other growth. Thus when he reached man but little of it was left, not enough to enable him to live eternally, sprouting up again like the trees; but still enough to enable him to recover from attacks of illness, when not too severe. But the trees and plants upon which it fell were benefited by it as man would have been, and that is why we see them renewing their life as they do."

FOLK-LORE FROM AFRICA

SEDDEE

Seddee was wounded, but neglected to dress his wound. Some of his friends asked him why he did not care for it, saying that such neglect would result in his death. Seddee replied, "It is my wound, and it will be my death." Hence the word "Seddee" among the Bassas means, "Attend to your own business."

WHY THE NATIVES DO NOT WEAR CLOTHES

In explaining why the natives do not wear clothing, an old native man relates this incident:

"Once," he says, "a big king sent to call all the different people of the world to meet at a certain place, that he might tell them of something. The day was cold and rainy, and the native man would not leave the fire in his rude hut to respond to the king's call.

"But all who did go to the king's court were taught to wear clothes, and were given books and fine houses as a reward for their obedience. Those who thought it too cold and rainy, and were not thus favored, remain unclad until this day."

MISSIONARY STORY SKETCHES

WAR WITH THE BABOONS

Once there was in a town a baby whose body was covered with craw craw, a very troublesome and unsightly skin disease. The mother of this child was compelled to work very hard on the rice farm, and owing to the condition of the little one's body she could not strap it upon her back, as is the usual custom, and take it with her to the field. She had to leave it in the hut uncared for and alone.

When all the people of the town had gone to their farms, a baboon who lived with a family of baboons in the nearby bush came into the town and soon found the afflicted baby. It took the child in its arms and carried it to the creek, where it bathed its wounds and anointed them with medicine made from roots and herbs. This was done with tenderest care. The baby was then taken back to the hut where its mother had left it, and this performance was repeated for several days.

The mother, returning from the farm and finding that her sick baby had been well cared for, was surprised, and as this kind treatment continued day after day, she resolved to hide herself and watch for the kind nurse. She had not long to wait, for as soon as the people had left the town and the baby was alone, the baboon came, took the baby in her arms, and cared for it as she had been doing.

FOLK-LORE FROM AFRICA

The next morning the father of the child watched for the baboon; she soon appeared and, emerging from the bush, made a direct line for the hut. The father was terrified and, as soon as the animal was near enough, shot the poor thing, painfully wounding her.

The baboon dragged its bleeding and mangled body with difficulty into the bush and there uttered loud and pitiful cries which told of its pain. This soon brought her mate and companions near. They were angry as they saw how her kindness had been rewarded.

The baboons gathered in large numbers, determined to avenge the wrong inflicted upon their innocent and suffering companion. They armed themselves with wild gourds, made war upon the town, driving all the people away, and it was never again inhabited.

The story contains a moral: Kindness should be accepted and rewarded in like spirit.

THE LEOPARD AND THE DOG

A long time ago all the animals of the forest agreed to have a great celebration among themselves, with music and dancing, to commemorate a historic event in the annals of wild beast existence. A banner of leaves and branches, garlanded with flowers and vines, was to be borne at the head of the procession by the largest animal.

In making their plans they found that they did not have a drum for the occasion, nor could they borrow one from anywhere. The leopard at once suggested to the assembly that each animal contribute from his own body a piece of skin to make the checkered head of the drum. This proposition was considered a wise one by the older heads of the forest, and was immediately adopted as the only solution of the difficulty.

Each animal readily complied with the requirements, and the dog was appointed custodian of the contributions. He happily and proudly assumed his task as watchman. But as the bits of skin lay in the tropical sun, undergoing their process of preparation, their smell and sight became more and more tempting, and the dog found it impossible to resist tasting one of the pieces. Having tasted one piece, he continued tasting piece after piece until he had eaten nearly all of the skins.

The leopard, who had charge of the making of the drum, came to look at the skins and found, to his utter surprise and disappointment, the dog gluttonously eating them; in fact, he had eaten nearly all. The leopard flew into a rage, sprang upon the dog, and gave him a terrible beating. Afterwards he chained the dog, making him his slave. The leopard then called all the beasts of the forest together to look upon the dog thus in disgrace. In course of time, however, the dog managed to snap a link of his chain and made good his escape into the wide world.

Before his death the leopard gathered his children around him and had them pledge enmity to the dog, promising to pounce upon and destroy him whenever and wherever found. And from that day the dog has been known as the leopard's slave, and they are inveterate enemies.

During the time the leopard had the dog chained, the dog saw the whelps of the leopard's daughter, the lioness. Cats bear such a strong resemblance to these young lions, the dog imagines cats to be the leopard's grandchildren. Having no friendship for the leopard, he is ever ready for a fight when he encounters cats.

Moral: The fruit of dishonesty is a lasting pestilence.

ELEPHANT, HIPPOPOTAMUS, AND TORTOISE

Elephant, hippopotamus, and the tortoise were once upon a time great friends. But one day, when the tortoise was walking near a river with the elephant, he saw a chance to cunningly outwit his big friend, and accordingly told the elephant that, many times bigger as he was, he could nevertheless pull him into the water close by.

This amused the elephant greatly, and with derisive laughter he told the tortoise that the suggestion was preposterous. But the little tortoise, all the more determined to put into execution his plan, urged him to let him try, and when the elephant scornfully consented he fastened a rope about his body and bade him remain where he was until he pulled him in, after which he walked with the other end of the rope to the river.

There he told his friend the hippopotamus that, though he was many times larger, he could pull him out of the water. The hippopotamus was astonished at the audacity of the statement and sarcastically told the tortoise to try it. Whereupon tortoise, with inward glee, fastened the second end of the rope about him and told him to get into the water and pull, which he did.

The elephant, feeling the strain on the rope, resisted it as hard as he could, and thus the two unwitting combatants worked furiously until they were too tired to pull any longer. Then, each incredulous that the tortoise could have pulled so hard, they slowly followed the rope to see. Thus they walked up to each other and discovered the deceit that had been practiced upon them, when they felt very foolish and consequently became angry and swore to kill the tortoise wherever they found him.

FOLK-LORE FROM AFRICA

THE TORTOISE AND THE PIG

Once when there was a great famine the tortoise had nothing to eat, and in order to cut some dates he climbed up into a palm tree, but he lost his balance when he reached the top and fell to the ground. He fell on his back, and his shell was broken into pieces.

He lay there helpless till all the animals were returning home at evening, and as each one passed he beseeched him to gather the pieces of his shell for him. But one after another refused, until the pig passed, and he was prevailed upon to collect the shell and put the tortoise in it. For this service the pig was promised a reward on a certain day.

When the day arrived he went to the home of the tortoise, where he found Mrs. Tortoise grinding some leaves on a stone, as he thought. She told him that her husband was out, which made the pig angry. In his ill-humor he pushed away the stone, which really was the tortoise himself, lying on his back. He then left; and when he returned the second time the tortoise agreed to pay him when he found the stone he had pushed away from Mrs. Tortoise.

So the pig went to look for the stone, and has not found it yet, of course. And that is why the pig goes grunting along the ground to this

MISSIONARY STORY SKETCHES

day, and that is why the back of the tortoise is cracked.

TORTOISE'S CREDITORS

Once upon a time a famine was in the land, and the tortoise sat down to think of some cunning scheme to help him in his destitute state. As a result of his planning he went to his friends: the worm, cock, wild cat, leopard, and hunter, and from each of them borrowed seven boxes of brass rods. These he promised to pay on different days at the end of the season, telling the worm to come first for his money, the cock next, and so on; the hunter being last.

When the time agreed upon came, the worm went to him for payment. But the tortoise told him to wait, saying he had to go to fetch the money. So the worm waited; and the next day the tortoise came back, followed by the cock, whose payment was now due. Seeing the worm, the cock swallowed him up, and then told the tortoise the object of his visit.

But the tortoise told the cock likewise to wait while he got the money; and when he returned, the wild cat came with him and devoured the cock. When he then asked for his money he was told to wait, while the tortoise went out for it.

This time the leopard came back with the tortoise, and he, seeing the wild cat, fell upon him and killed him, after which he explained the reason for his coming; and he, as the others had been, was told to wait, which he did in ignorance of the cunning he was so soon to fall a prey to.

Shortly the tortoise came back, and with him the hunter, who fired at the leopard, though he failed to kill him. So the leopard attacked him, and they fought until they both were dead. Their corpses were then used by the wicked tortoise, who laughed at the foolishness of his victims.

Therefore we should not lend our money to any man, as he would try to get rid of us, in order to be able to keep our money.

THE SPIDER AND THE PWEH

The common spider is an emblem of chicanery, and a spirit whose name is Pweh represents justice among the Bassas.

The spider got inside a ram's skin, that was sewed up so as to represent or imitate a sheep and was led away by his companions for sale.

Pweh desired to purchase the animal to eat, but as it did not look quite natural, he suspected cheating somewhere and, to verify or disprove his surmises, proposed to butcher the supposed animal, and pay for it afterward.

MISSIONARY STORY SKETCHES

The spider, hearing the proposition and fearing detection, murmured hoarsely inside the skin, "Let's go; can't make a bargain; can't make a bargain." So the false sheep was led away.

The use of the words of the spider, "Can't make a bargain," in making a trade, is usually regarded as chicanery.

THE FOOLISH SHEEP

One day long ago all the animals fixed themselves up in their very best suits, for all were invited to a big dance in a neighboring town. But though all looked very fine, none looked better than the pretty sheep, who wore for the first time a beautiful white woolen dress.

But very foolishly she allowed her vanity to overcome her discretion, and in order to show her suit she disported and danced nearly all the way, and thus used up all her strength.

Following the custom of the Gedoboes, the animals bathed after their traveling as soon as they reached the town. But the sheep danced around even after the others had gone to bathe, and only ceased at the last moment, so that upon her return from her bath she trembled on her limbs from over-exhaustion, and while the others started in to enjoy the festivities, feeling fresh and rested, she had to withdraw.

And from this incident arose the parable the Gedoboes have: "Do not play until your time comes."

THE ELEPHANT AND THE GOAT

Current among the natives of the interior of Liberia is a story about the elephant and the goat. They say that once the elephant and the goat decided to have a contest to see which could eat the more. The elephant, being so much larger than the goat, was sure of winning. He laughed at the presumption of the goat.

The contest began. The elephant greedily tore up grass and weeds, and ate voraciously until he could eat no more. The goat ate leisurely, and then lay down upon a rock and began chewing his cud.

"Why," said the elephant, "I thought you were through. What are you eating now?"

"I am eating this rock that I am lying on," replied the goat, "and when I finish it, I am going to eat you."

The elephant was very much frightened and until this day thinks the goat means to carry out his awful threat. For this reason he never lingers in the goat's presence.

MISSIONARY STORY SKETCHES

The natives, when traveling along through the section of country which is the habitat of the elephants, always take with them a goat, and the above narrative is the reason they give for this custom. As a matter of fact, the peculiar noise of the nanny goats frightens the elephant, and he loses no time in running away.

LEGENDS TOLD BY A QUARTET OF KROO "BOYS"

Woore's Tale.—A long time ago the sun did not shine, so 't was always night. In the forest there stood a tree which far exceeded in height any other; and "so it was" that so long as this tree stood there could be no day. Therefore all the beasts of the forest conspired to pull it down. The elephant, confident in his strength, first tried; but tried in vain. After him the lion, leopard, and many other animals worked hard, but all to no purpose; none could pull it down or root it up. At last, when all the others had despaired of accomplishing their object, the little "Nuh" (an animal resembling the ferret), came forward and told them that he was stronger than they all, and would soon prove it by felling the tree. So off he ran, but soon returned with a small but sharp hatchet, with which he cut away till the tree fell, and as it fell the sun rose for the first time.

FOLK-LORE FROM AFRICA

Seah's Tale.—Once an elephant got a stick long enough to reach "Big America," put it into the water, and gave notice to all other animals that he who would cross over to America on that stick and bring back from there a leaf should marry his daughter. One after another attempted to cross: lions, tigers, bush-cats, baboons, and even monkeys; but none could walk far before the stick would roll over and let them into the water. By and by "Nuh" walked softly upon the stick, crossed over to America, and brought back a leaf, which he gave to the elephant, and he in return gave him his daughter, as was promised.

Keah's Story (Native Version).—First time all dem meat (wild beasts) he make one big town, tiger be king, for de little fish dem people kill. Tiger take em every bit, so he can't get notting. So he can't kill fish agin, and all dem people say, "Which way; fus time we live here we eat plenty fish, how come dis time we can't eat none?" So he take "Nuh" he go for dotor, and tell him all he palaver, and dotor say, "Very well; no make tiger be king for you town. Spose tiger be king, nobody can't eat notting no more. You must make little meat (Nuh) king for you town." So he make him king. Plenty fish die, and tiger eat him, and "Nuh" gete mad and go nother place for sit he down. Tiger send people go call him, so all can sit down one place. No more he say,

MISSIONARY STORY SKETCHES

"Let tiger have him place, me I can't go dere." So all dem meat say, "S'pose you can't go, we can't go too." And tiger left alone him town. Bimeby tiger self get up and go for call "Nuh," but he no will for go him place. So tiger want to fight, and "Nuh," too, he want to fight. No more all two fear togeder, and run away. Since dat time all dem meat live walk all about.

Djuabie's Story.—Years ago there lived in Bush country a very handsome young woman named Jarwee. Many a young man vainly sought her hand, and she seemed perfectly indifferent to all. Crowrock, hearing of her, determined to possess her or die. So, taking his boy, he journeyed till he reached her home, and, presenting himself as a suitor, asked for her handkerchief to wipe himself with, and entreated her to be his wife; but she would not listen to him, and he, becoming quite desperate, declared if she would not have him he would throw himself into the fire. Still she did not appear to heed his entreaties; and he was about to execute his threat when her mother and friends interposed, exclaiming: "Po-po-ke-en-keh! (Don't burn yourself.) Po-po-ke-en-keh! You shall have her. She shall be your wife, and you can carry her to your home." Then the mother cooked him rice, gave him water to wash, and the daughter became his wife.

FOLK-LORE FROM AFRICA

NATIVE PARABLES

If a man calls you and you refuse to answer, you will be driven to reply if he persists in calling you.

Meaning: Perseverance conquers difficulty.

Smoked meat is sweet; but what will you have to eat in the meanwhile, before the meat is thus prepared?

Meaning: A bird in the hand is better than a thousand in the bushes.

Might and strength simply can not produce wealth.

Meaning: Prosperity is heaven's gift.

Drain you the crab-hole ever so dry, there will be drops of water found in it still.

Meaning: Be a man ever so poor, still he has some property or other to boast of, something to call his own.

In the absence of the leopard the dog trespasses in its den or cave.

Meaning: Your bitterest or weakest foe will take advantage of your absence.

If a man live long enough, he shall have eaten as much as a whole elephant.

Meaning: Long life furnishes a chance to achieve great things.

MISSIONARY STORY SKETCHES

The rain that falls on the master can fall on his slave too.

Meaning: Trouble is no respecter of persons.

If the rat that walks about in the day fall into a trap, how more liable to be caught are those who walk about in the night?

Meaning: If they do these things in a green tree, what will be done in the dry?

If raindrops fail to fill the bucket, dewdrops can not fill it.

Meaning: If those who are in every way qualified to perform an office fail to execute it, it is highly presumptive in others who possess fewer of such qualifications to dream of their ability to accomplish the task.

It was the sudden fall of rain that obliged goats and sheep to rush together in one place.

Meaning: "What can't be cured must be endured."

Cockroaches have no protection of their lives in a country inhabited by fowls.

Meaning: When in the enemy's land, never reckon you are safe.

After you get to the large cotton tree you see yonder you now admire, you will not think too much more of it.

Meaning: "Satiety follows after full possession."

FOLK-LORE FROM AFRICA

If you engage a bad woman in a public dancing-room to be your wife, you both are in danger of separation when you attend some other dance subsequently.

Meaning: If you marry a divorced woman, take care you don't have to divorce her too.

If you say you will save one from any trouble, do it entirely.

Meaning: If you will save one from any distress, do it effectually, and do not afterward become antagonistic to him by sinking him into it the deeper.

If you are drowning in the sea, drink enough of its water at once.

Meaning: If you can't possibly remedy any danger to you, succumb by selling your life dearly.

"Jookoo" brings "Jakkah."

Meaning: Tit for tat; evil be to him who evil thinks.

A polygamist must have plenty of common sense to cope with the members of his harem.

Meaning: One who has taken many responsibilities upon himself must have sufficient tact and means to square up with them.

MISSIONARY STORY SKETCHES

You are not the alligator's brother after all your best swimming in the water by its side.

Meaning: A foreigner is but a foreigner, say what you please, do what you may.

The small elephant has large tusks.

Meaning: Great events hang on small things.

The frog thought there was no other sort of water in the world but the cold and comfortable kind in which he was reared; but circumstances brought it about one day so that he tumbled into boiling water. All frogs learned then a lesson from this sad but well-bought experience of their unfortunate companion; hence their significant screeching noise near ponds and swamps at night, saying, "Water is more than one kind." Response, "More than one; more than one."

Meaning: The wealthy heir thinks there is nothing but happiness and prosperity in life; but when suddenly overtaken by adversity he and his friends are taught the useful lesson that life is checkered.

One finger does not pick out the vermin in your head.

Meaning: "Two are better than one."

If money brings love into the house, it will carry it back when it returns.

Meaning: If we love for the sake of wealth, we shall hate when poverty comes.

FOLK-LORE FROM AFRICA

SOME AFRICAN (LIBERIAN) PROVERBS

The leopard says: If a thing is running, it is food.

The G'de (monkey) says: It must be knowledge, it is not large. (Knowledge is better than size.)

The Gbubudugba (plant) says: If I have no sower I sow myself.

The squirrel says: For wisdom's sake two people walk (together).

The red ant says: If you are (nearly) consumed, you enter into one nest (in peace).

The bush rat says: If you rest, you eat your tail (from want).

Stopping (hindering) another, thou stoppest thyself.

The foot that walks the road, that one a thorn strikes.

I have a vessel already; then why should I search for one to put things in?

The ox says: Given leaves do not satisfy.

Before you can make soup you must have the meat.

Whatever, a snake appearing, is at hand, with that he kills it.

If you want to catch fish, do n't shake the water.

A strange cock does not crow.

MISSIONARY STORY SKETCHES

Money is a gentleman's slave.

When the elephant died as a visitor, he made but one load (because of his leanness).

If thou alone are left in the world, thou art to be pitied.

The hen says: We walk after him that has something.

Where the head is not, there is the back (also poverty).

Pull the child out of the water before you punish it.

If nothing troubles you, you are unborn.

The snail says: I should tell it, but I have no foot for running. (It is not safe to tell a secret if you can not run away.)

The hand-thing is sweet (*i. e.*, a thing gained by work).

The guinea pig says: One does not cross the water talking.

One does not esteem suppositions.

The guinea fowl says: One does not risk life for show.

The gazelle says: Wisdom is life.

The big monkey says: Word does not prevent word.

"Softly, softly," killed the monkey.

One palm spoils all the wine (if it is bad).

The crab says: If you meet others in the mud,

then go into mud (for there must be some danger near).

The red ant says: The world is large, yet you hear no noise.

The crocodile says: The water is very long (far), but the canoe lands (at last).

"I only may eat, another must eat"—this carried the hedgehog to the bush (*i. e.*, he was driven out).

The "rained on" musk deer says: If you leave your place you do not find a (dry) place.

The wild goat says: Morning food is blood. (Early hours make one prosper.)

The lizard says: If you have nothing, you make a hunchback (*i. e.*, you walk dejectedly).

The small ant says: Nothing beats a crowd.

A snake curled up eats nothing.

The devil-fish (very ugly) says: Men's faces are unlike.

The monkey ate with two hands, and fell from the tree.

The fox says: The pit of safety is not deep.

The stork says: Nothing hurts a child of light.

The (big-headed) fish says: Your head must grow before you ascend the river (*i. e.*, you need sense before you travel).

The crocodile says: One does not carry the bowels to market.

Broken things last long.

III

NATIVE INCIDENTS AND ITEMS
1. From Social Life
2. From Religious Life

NATIVE INCIDENTS AND ITEMS FROM SOCIAL LIFE

MISSION WARRED UPON BY CANNIBALS

When a discouraged missionary asks himself, "After all, what progress has been made?" he need only remember the condition of Liberia sixty years or so ago and compare it to to-day. To establish a mission then meant the imminent risk of being warred upon by cannibalistic tribes and "eaten for breakfast," which was the specific threat made by King Gotarah in 1840 to George S. Brown, who founded the Heddington Mission, five hours from Monrovia.

Before daybreak one morning in March of that year the inmates of the mission were awakened by the firing of a musket about a half mile distant. Cries of "War in the path!" resounded through the woods, and were found to have been uttered by an old woman, who made her way to King Thom, near the mission, and told him that a large congregation of war people were near at hand.

MISSIONARY STORY SKETCHES

Before she finished speaking their muskets could be seen in the early faint light of daybreak, and it was discerned that they were in three divisions: one on guard, the other two surrounding the town en march. The wings, when fired upon, returned to the body; but not without a return fire, which wounded one of the missionaries so that he died, though conscious to the last, and dying happy in Jesus; he was a converted native.

Mr. Brown had in his mission twenty-six school children, two hired girls, and the wife of an American man, Harris; he being there also, and helpful in resisting the attacks of the enemy, taking an active initiative in the tactics employed by the mission party. Demory, another American, was of the group, and three of the boys were old enough to handle muskets. Thom and twelve of his men had muskets.

When the women and children tried to escape they were almost captured by the slave-catchers, and only with difficulty regained the mission, where Brown ordered them to go to one of the bedrooms and lie upon the floor, so that they might escape the firing as much as possible.

The enemy's slugs and balls flew thick and fast through Brown's house, aimed by four or five hundred almost at hand.

Demory and Harris, who happened to have

FOLK-LORE FROM AFRICA

four or five pounds of buckshot, stood below in front of the enemy, and Jarvis and Nichols at the window above, firing muskets as fast as a boy could hand them and another boy return them to Brown for loading.

A frail picket fence, whose weakness the enemy did not guess, held them back until sun up, when old Gotarah got behind the storehouse and smashed through the fence there. With yells he led his men on to within two rods of the house, and then, attempting to rush in, fell lifeless on the very threshold.

This ended the attack; and well it did, for the mission ammunition was exhausted to within a round or two.

This attack and its repulse ended the wars in that vicinity and did much to encourage the natives to lay out farms, as they no longer feared being driven off.

CANNIBALISM OF OLD TIMES IN LIBERIA

The question of cannibalism on the coast of Liberia was incidentally raised at the session of the Liberia Conference, in 1842, held in Monrovia. Rev. Anthony D. Williams, a member of the Conference, was presiding.

MISSIONARY STORY SKETCHES

The fact of cannibalism was denied by one of the preachers, who said "there never were cannibals known on the western coast of Africa."

Elijah Johnson, one of the founders of Liberia, whose experiences with the infant republic were many and thrilling, was well prepared to throw light on the subject. He said, "There certainly are cannibals on this coast, and I have seen them bring human flesh into Monrovia for sale, since I have lived here; fried or smoked human flesh."

Rev. J. W. Roberts, who afterwards became bishop for Liberia, testified to the same fact, saying that while he had not seen human flesh in Monrovia, he had seen it among the natives in their towns carried about in "kinjars" (native baskets made of thatch and bamboo) strapped to their backs.

Gaytoombay's general, Gotarah, sent the following message to Governor Buchanan: "I am a very bad man; my fashion is to take and burn a town, kill and eat people."

Gaytoombay was a powerful native chief, with whom the colonists contended in the early days of the republic. He was a veteran slave-trader, and was present when Captain Stockton and Dr. Ayers purchased Perseverance Island for the colonists.

FOLK-LORE FROM AFRICA

AN AVERTED WAR

The Hague Peace Conference, a mile-post leading to the highest civilization of the nations, presents a marked contrast to the heathen tribes of Africa, who, in their pitiable ignorance, quarrel and make senseless war upon one another on the slightest pretext; and only as mission work wields its influence does this instinct come under control, and the tribes learn to live without that constant fear, the one for the other.

Two or three years ago the people of the Garraway Mission in Liberia averted such a war between the Garraway and Po River tribes only after repeated efforts.

And the cause of the trouble was nothing more than the straying of a young bullock into the province of the river tribe. Because none owned it they concluded that the Garraway tribe had been to the "devil doctor," obtained from him war medicine, and put it upon the animal, that it might carry death to them.

This was the complaint they made to the two men sent by the mission at the coercion of the people, who reproached them for not protecting them, and this was the only reason they gave for having threatened war by blowing horns and cursing on the river bank all the preceding night. They exempted the mission people from all blame, however.

MISSIONARY STORY SKETCHES

When the men returned they found that the bullock had been sent back, and that the explanation had been given the Po River people that the King Gouh had given the women a cow, that they might have a dinner and dance in his honor; but when the soldiers tried to catch the cow she ran into the bushes, this little calf following her; and when they captured the king's gift they left the calf, which swam across the Po River to the other town. They also gave the messengers who returned the calf, cloth, rum, and other gifts.

But later in the day the peace offerings were returned, with another proclamation of war. As angry words multiplied across the river, the mission people again endeavored to cast oil upon the troubled waters; but when they attempted to make the same explanation concerning the bullock, which —poor, dumb animal!—knew not what a mountain of wrath it had evoked by its innocent wandering, the Po River tribe declared the mission people, too, lied and were as bad as the heathen.

The messengers returned heavy-hearted and were close followed by a messenger, who said: "I am the last man now to cross this river. I am come to shake the dust off my feet, and you will never again see any of our people across this river."

The general of the Po River, who had been banished for a year, returned within a few days and sent word to the Garraway king that he was waiting to shake his hand. And yet again other messengers, to declare that the two tribes were friends and allies, and that, it being time to go and cut farms, they trusted the Garraway people to care for their women and children during their absence.

And so the poor heathen, in the folly of their mistaken traditions and beliefs, ever seek to show their courage by their readiness to assume arms, working themselves up over such a trivial incident into a rage which is bitter while it lasts.

THE FEROCITY AND INTREPIDITY OF AN AFRICAN CHIEF

Captain Cano, whose adventures among the natives in Cape Mount are told by himself in a book written with graphic power of description and filled with thrilling incidents, tells of a remarkable incident which illustrates the ferocity of an African chief in the days of the African slave trade.

The chief, Fano Toro, who was seventy-seven years of age, ruled over six towns and fifteen villages. He was of small stature, but of erect carriage and of a nervous temperament. In youth he was famous for barbarity, cherishing bitter enmity toward foes, and practicing upon them crimes shocking to humanity.

Upon one occasion when he visited the chief, Cano says that he found him in a palaver house with his subjects silently gathered about him. He had succeeded in capturing his bitterest and oldest foe, who had been for twenty years an intolerable menace to him and his tribe, burning his towns, butchering and selling his people, and slaying his sons.

But now his enemy was at last caught and slain by him, and his victim lay stretched upon the ground, in the palaver house, and Toro, with his foot planted upon the carcas and a bloody knife in his hand, was addressing it. He recounted with inflamed passion the numerous wrongs committed against him and his people by the dead chief, and with each sentence he plunged the cruel blade into the lifeless frame. Beside him was a large pot of hissing oil, in which was frying the heart of his old antagonist. Having thus vented his spleen and appeased his wrath on the remains, he ordered that the body be burned to prevent the spirit of the dead man from haunting him the balance of his days.

Toro suffered many annoyances from marauding and mercenary bands, who under the leadership of rival chiefs united against him to utterly despoil him and his tribe. On one occasion they besieged his stockade for many days. His men remained loyal and valiant, and rallied around their resolute chief as long as possible, until they were absolutely emaciated by hunger and thirst, and unable to resist longer. Their only remedy was surrender. This Toro stoutly refused to consider, preferring death to yielding to his enemies.

With despairing energy he strode into the palaver house, and with the port of a born commander ordered all to sally forth upon his beleaguers. His fainting, starving warriors, with supplies and ammunition exhausted, disobeyed the order and counseled displacing him and naming a successor, which was done.

Toro, lashed to anger by this stubborn resistance and contempt of his commands, in his humiliation defied his successor to equal him in his power of endurance, and, to demonstrate this, plunged his finger in a boiling pot of oil, and then placed it in the flames until it was burned to a black, charred crisp, remaining all the while unmoved.

His tribe, seeing this, cheered wildly and rescinded their action, restoring him as chief. Seizing this favorable opportunity, Toro rallied his men and routed his enemy. The burned finger was ever afterwards a souvenir of the victory of the chief and his people.

MISSIONARY STORY SKETCHES

THE CONSTABLE AND THE ZOE-VLENG

When once placed within the sacred precincts of the Gri-Gri Bush, under the care of the Zoe-vleng, usually no native power can interfere with the members. With this fact well known, a man caught a young woman along the highway and took her to the Zoe-vleng for safe-keeping. She was one of the wives of a debtor of his, and, having had difficulty in collecting a long-standing debt with the man, he adopted this method of recovering it.

The matron of the grove was a free widow and had a village of her own near the Gri-Gri Bush. The town where the chief of the district lived was about a half mile away.

The woman's husband entered a suit against his creditors for kidnaping his wife, and the constable proceeded with a squad of his men to the village to reclaim the woman. The guide pointed out the woman, in order that the constable might arrest her, but the matron ordered her into the house.

The old woman resorted to her rattle, which gave a tremendous alarm. One of the men, who knew its meaning, informed the officer that the Zoe-vleng was calling for help, and advised that the rattle be taken from her. This was done, and it was thrown away, when the woman began to scream distressfully.

FOLK-LORE FROM AFRICA

"Scream on," said the officer. "You are obstructing my writ, and I shall take you along with me," and he made it quite plain to the woman who he was.

The men laid hold of each hand and started off with her on a run. They knew that the alarm was sure to bring help to her; so they lost no time in clearing out of the way of her rescuers. But the old woman made up her mind to resist authority as long as possible.

She fell sprawling on the ground; but they dragged her at a running pace over the gravel, rocks, and roots, while she cried, "Let me up, and I'll walk."

"We do n't want you to walk; we want you to run!" they said.

"O, then I'll run; anything, only let me up," she pleaded, piteously.

She was allowed to arise, but she refused to walk, thinking to delay them until assistance arrived.

The men gave her a vigorous jerk and started off again.

Finding they were determined, she scrambled up, and rather than be dragged again she trotted off again in good earnest.

Thus for five miles along a rough road she continued to run until they reached the canoes. They knew that, if overtaken, her high position would provoke an attack from the natives. They had just cleared the wharf when the pursuers appeared on the bank with their big knives and spears.

The men declared they had never had such a run in their lives before, neither did the Zoe-vleng. She was much chagrined to find herself a prisoner. What a forlorn figure she did present! Such a position for the head of the Gri-Gri Bush was pathetic.

The judge, however, was lenient with her, for she was a heathen woman and unacquainted with higher laws than those of her bush.

The man's wife was restored to him.

A MAN IN THE GRI-GRI BUSH

The Gri-Gri Bush is a sealed grove especially for women, and men are strictly forbidden to enter there. The following incident is an account of a tradesman's experience with the bush while in session.

He was making a trading tour in the interior, having a number of carriers with him, who were loaded with merchandise. Arriving in a strange part of the country, both trader and carriers missed their way, and coming suddenly upon what was supposed to be a village, the trader entered, but to his astonishment and also his exceeding discomfiture found that it was Gri-Gri Bush.

ZOE-VLENGS, OR PRECEPTRESSES, OF THE GRI-GRI BUSH IN OFFICIAL COSTUME.

[The Gri-Gri Bush is a cloistered institution for females where they receive instruction in all those things which fall into the sphere of womanhood. The bush is located in the forest in a secluded grove some little distance from the dwellings and farms. The grounds are carefully marked off, and are considered sacred. Men are strictly forbidden to enter the enclosure. An elderly woman, a sort of governess or preceptress, has charge of the girls who enter there between the ages of ten and twelve, where they remain for a number of years until the prescribed work is finished.]

FOLK-LORE FROM AFRICA

The Zoe-vleng instantly made an alarm by seizing the rattle, which is a large gourd enclosed in a network of beads, and giving a few vigorous jerks. The women at this distress signal wildly rushed from the huts and pounced upon the intruder, and before he could fully realize his situation he found himself in the clutches of infuriated women and fast bound.

By this time the men had gathered and learned from the carriers the state of affairs. They hailed the women, telling them not to harm their prisoner, for he was a stranger and had entered there through mistake. By this timely interference the frightened trader escaped a severe flogging. However, the unforgiving women retained their prisoner, threatening to kill him outright unless he paid a heavy fine. He shouted to his carriers to give them the kinjars of merchandise. These were handed over as a peace offering, and the unfortunate man was very glad to escape with his life.

BETTIE

Meeting a heathen woman far up in the interior with a heavy load of wood on her head, and seeing a large scar on her shoulder, I was anxious to know who she was and how she came to receive such an ugly wound. She seemed to appreciate the interest shown and, instantly dropping

MISSIONARY STORY SKETCHES

her wood, said that her name was Bettie. She had been one of the wives of a chief of the Pessey tribe who had been conquered and killed in war, and was now one of the wives of her husband's slayer, according to heathen usage.

The scar on her shoulder, to which she pointed with tears in her eyes, was given her by the warrior who captured her. She was not easy to take, and during the struggle an attempt was made to behead her. Dodging, the sword missed her head and made the ugly mark on her shoulder, which she will always bear. Bettie was the mother of five children, but they had all died by poisoning. She was an object which stirred the deepest pity as she told her sad story.

IN STICKS

There are many methods of punishment, all more or less cruel, among the natives in the interior, for crimes committed and for other misdemeanors.

One of the most practiced modes of torture is that of putting the culprit in sticks. A green log from three to five feet in length and eight to twelve inches in diameter is prepared and brought into the palaver house. A hole is made in the center of the log large enough to thrust the foot through, and if the crime is of sufficient greatness, two holes are made and both feet are put through. The victim is compelled to bear this punishment, sometimes for many months, until confession is made of the crime for which it is applied, or until the ends of justice are met.

Passing through a town one day we saw a woman with one foot in the stick; she was suffering intensely from the pain caused by the swelling of the entire limb. She had been placed there for some trifling offense, but there was no redress for her. Native law is strict and unrelenting.

At the sight of our party those who were administering punishment to the woman began to cut the log with an ax. But as we made no protest, and passed on, they soon stopped, and the woman remained a prisoner.

EXECUTION AND OTHER PENALTIES

There obtains no particular method of executing criminals among the aborigines except those condemned in the devil bush tribunal. These are taken in the dense forest, bound hand and foot, laid flat upon their stomach, with neck resting upon a large pole laid on the ground; with a club the executioner then strikes the culprit three heavy blows on the back of the neck, which leaves him dead. Or sometimes they are placed upon their backs, a stout stick laid upon their throats, upon each end of which a man sits until the victim suffocates, which is generally within a few minutes.

In most other cases prisoners are delivered over to such persons as are willing to kill them—which are always readily found among the heathen—and they cruelly cut them up until death ensues, cutting from the body hands, arms, ears, and other members, ofttimes stabbing, running swords through the body, slicing from fleshy parts, and so on, until the unfortunate victim expires under these horrors.

Where civilized law operates, this sort of punishment is not permissible. Those guilty of crime are duly tried and humanely punished. Happily this latter method is steadily spreading among the heathen.

DAMAGES

Injuries or losses, whether accidental or intentional, are recoverable. Even slight accidents have occasioned serious palavers, and payments of damages called for. The claim of parents and relatives upon their children is peculiar, and especially so with reference to the girls. Marriage does not relinquish the claim. Losses occasioned by the death of a wife may be recovered under a custom known as "redeeming the body." This claim can

FOLK-LORE FROM AFRICA

be annulled only by the mutual consent of the parents and a second party.

If a father buys a wife for his son while yet a minor, paying the legal price, and the woman dies before she becomes his wife, her parents present claims for redeeming the dead body. If the claim is met, a responsibility is attached to the parents or relatives of the deceased to furnish another wife for the boy, whom he marries when of age, paying the usual dowry. Sometimes a servant is included.

Failure to redeem the corpse of a wife cancels the right to claim the children who may have been born of that wife. Redeeming the dead body of a woman who was a mother, involves a greater expense than a woman who died without offspring.

HEATHEN SYMPATHY

The most delicate and genuine expression of sympathy that we have ever seen was extended by a heathen woman who called on a Liberian woman recently bereaved of an only son. The mother, overwhelmed with grief, was reclining upon a cot, seemingly oblivious of her surroundings. Friends had gathered to comfort her, and they filled the room. It seemed difficult to find appropriate words to condole with the afflicted mother, whose grief was twofold, for she had only recently suffered the loss of a loving husband.

In such a presence silence seemed more appropriate than words. The native woman was of the Vey tribe. Softly she crept into the room, and tenderly kneeling down by the woman's side, with her face to the floor, she gently took hold of the widow's foot and placed it against her cheek. She patted the foot with caressing strokes in silence for some minutes.

Then, rising from her position and looking at the woman with kindly, wistful eyes, amid her tears and with quivering lips, in her own tongue said, simply, "Never mind, mammy; never mind!"

Like the woman in Dickens's "Bleak House," "she had no kind of grace about her but the grace of sympathy; but when she condoled with the woman, and her own tears fell, she wanted no beauty."

AS TOLD BY DAVID KELLY

David Kelly and his wife, together with fifty or more persons known as the Liberian Enterprise Company, from the State of Pennsylvania, emigrated to Liberia in 1853. They carried with them machinery and merchandise to the amount of several thousand dollars in value. One of their several ventures was to install a twelve-horsepower sawmill at Marshall.

FOLK-LORE FROM AFRICA

This, however, after a brief existence, proved unsuccessful, the heavy expense of erecting and maintaining the mill making it impossible to continue it, and the scheme was ultimately abandoned. Kelly afterwards established himself at White Plains, on the St. Paul's River, where he was engaged for a number of years as a missionary in the Methodist Mission. He tells the following incidents of his life there:

The first is an amusing experience a Golah man had with a mirror. He had come from the interior to get a job of cleaning off bush for farm purposes, and had occasion to go in a room where there was a looking-glass. He had never seen one before, and thus did not recognize the fact, when he stepped in the door, that the "other man" he saw to the right was his reflection, but imagined it to be a man outside.

He addressed the reflection in the Vey language and said, "Accouy O?" (How do, my countryman?); but receiving no response, he repeated his salutation.

Being a second time ignored, he went out and searched diligently for the man in the place where he thought he had seen him. Not finding him there, he was confused. He returned again to the room and, looking in the mirror, beheld the same man where he had first seen him. Mystified, he ventured another greeting to the phantom, in the most respectful manner, but, of course, with no effect.

Excitedly he asked a Congo girl who was busy about the house what that man was doing there. She answered only with a smile, fully appreciating the joke. Failing to get an explanation, he crept stealthily to the door and threw a final sly glance at the mirror; then, leaving the work undone, in a spasm of fear he frantically hurried away, calling both legs and lungs into vigorous requisition in his flight. He was never seen about the mission again.

The second incident is quite as amusing and is one wherein a chart glass instead of a mirror played the mysterious rôle.

A Golah chief, seeing Mr. Kelly light his pipe with a chart glass, said, "Och! What side da fire can come?"

"From the sun," was the reply.

"Well, what's the matter the sun don't burn up all men?" said the astonished chief.

"That," said Mr. Kelly, "is because God has so arranged it that it warms and animates, but does not destroy life. When the rain falls in fine drops, nothing moves out of its place; but when the rain is gathered into larger and many drops, it tears things up by the roots.

"Now, heat from the sun is so finely divided

that like fine rain it affects nothing any further than is good for all God's creatures. This glass gathers the finely divided rays, and they are centered in one spot. So intense is the heat then that it has the power to burn, and to set tobacco on fire."

The chief listened intently and looked wise as the explanation proceeded, and at the close, said, "Umph, umph, umph! God have too much sense for true, true."

In illustrating what heathen customs obtain among the people, Mr. Kelly tells of a native man who carried a tumbler half full of rice to a large cotton tree that measured forty-three feet in circumference at the base. The tree was an object of worship, and the rice was a sacrificial offering to the dead and evil spirits who were believed to be hovering about the spot. Although the rats and field mice had a feast, the poor, deluded man believed that the dead feasted on his offering.

DEVOTION TO DUTY

It is customary among nearly all African tribes to have some sort of an institution among themselves for their girls and boys, where they perpetuate their tribal customs and prepare the young to become loyal men and women of the tribe.

MISSIONARY STORY SKETCHES

A number of families of the Vey tribe had migrated to the Gibi country, and they were there without these institutions for the perpetuation of the Vey customs. Jessa, though by no means a young woman, walked the distance of one hundred and twenty miles in four days to assist in setting up a Gri-Gri Bush for the girls of her tribe. She took with her tobacco to pay her way in providing food for herself in the strange towns through which she passed.

While she was in the Gibi country setting up this institution, word came to her of the serious illness of her granddaughter; she set out immediately to visit her afflicted relative. On the way she killed two birds with one stone, a deed which to her was a good omen. Her only compensation for establishing the bush and walking that long distance was the joy of service. She had served her tribe and obeyed the laws of her native community, and that was to her ample reward.

PARENTS BLESSING THEIR CHILDREN

Heathen parents have a custom of blessing their children. The parent who performs this ceremony usually sits down with the palms of both hands striking rapidly against his knees while pronouncing the blessing upon the child. Then they call upon the great, good spirit to grant the de-

GIRL MOTHER AND BABE.

sire of their heart and grant unto the child the blessing sought.

In the same manner they call upon the evil spirit to curse a child who is incorrigible and troublesome. They believe in the fulfillment of these blessings and curses. Young people who have been blessed by their parents often boast of the fact. Sometimes they will say, "My mother is beating her knees for me, and I must not do this wrong, as she has asked me not to do it."

An old man who brought his little son to the mission house said to me, "Keep my boy until he catch manhood, then bless him and put him away."

He thought if the missionary would bless the boy, no harm would ever befall him, and that everything he attempted to do would prosper: his cattle multiply, his farm yield abundantly, and that he would have a large family to perpetuate his name.

FEEDING BABIES

Newly born babies are fed by their mothers during the first few weeks of their existence on a little warm water or rice water. Then, as the baby gets older, this liquid diet is increased, in addition to the mother's milk. Later a little soft-boiled rice finely mashed is given in generous quantities. The older folks believe in eating large

MISSIONARY STORY SKETCHES

quantities, and follow the same plan with their children in early life.

By the time the baby is three or four months old the mother begins a new method of feeding. A bowl of palm butter and rice, with a generous supply of pepper, is then given. The baby is taken between the knees and stuffed with this until its stomach is distended to its uttermost capacity. Then it is thoroughly greased all over with nut oil from the palm nut, and placed upon its back in the sun, where it soon falls asleep.

When there is any difficulty in getting the baby to swallow, the mother gently presses the nostrils, compelling it to breathe through the mouth, and thus the act of swallowing is forced. Sometimes respiration is so long suspended that the mother inflates the lungs by blowing into the child's mouth. When told that her way of feeding the baby is not a good one, and attempting to introduce the use of a spoon, the heathen mother laughs at the idea and says the baby would starve to death if it had only what it could be induced to take in that manner.

SIGNIFICANCE OF AFRICAN NAMES

Names of native places and persons are not haphazardly given in Africa. Like names among the ancient Hebrews, they are suggested by some

FOLK-LORE FROM AFRICA

physical act or idea. The native name of Monrovia, "Dru-Kau," the capital of Liberia, is derived from its nearness to an abundance of water.

The following native towns in the interior are in keeping with the same rule: Guey zarto means to *sew up leaves;* Saw yonar, *top rock;* Zway bee, *ant bear hole.* The Doe Mountains in the Junk country, called by the Liberians "Galilee," are named by the natives from a kind of fish found in the streams near by. The fish is called by the natives *doe;* hence *Doe Mountains.* This antedates the name given by the Liberians.

The native name of Careysburg, an inland Americo-Liberian town, is Fawblee. It means *bullock's rest.* The natives, with their caravans from the interior, traveling to the St. Paul's River and the settlement of the colonists, always rested at this spot with their burdens and bullocks; hence the name.

The names of persons are similarly given: Jay Jay Nough, name of a powerful Gibi chief, means *sight to be seen devil.* Dwanh, means *to run.* The person received this name in war times, when his parents fled from the enemy at the time of his birth. Nawvlee, the name of one of the old kings of the Gibi country, means *big devil.* Bolah, a woman's name, means *cow's tail.*

African names are an interesting study and, always signifying thus something in native thought, have a force and beauty all their own. Missionaries, in changing children's names indiscriminately, destroy their identity with their tribes and homes. As a rule they ought not to be changed. Christian names may be easily added to the native name.

A KROO FUNERAL

A Krooman was taken ill very suddenly, and continued to grow worse until the fourth day, when he died. On the third night of his illness his friends took him from the hut in which he lay and carried him across the town to another house. This was done for two reasons; first, to defeat the evil spirits who would lurk around the dead man's spirit the moment it left his body; and second, to prevent them from causing his spirit to transmigrate into that of some dangerous beast or animal.

After his death his body was taken back to his hut, a new suit of clothes put upon it, and a dozen or more pieces of cloth, a hat, umbrella, shoes (he wore no shoes in life), and many other articles, such as handkerchiefs, bottles of Florida water, coins, etc., were placed upon his bier.

A canopy of sail cloth was stretched across the street, and the body with all its adornment placed in the middle of the street. The widows of the deceased were in the hut, seated on the ground, with only a scanty loin cloth around them. They were wailing and mourning bitterly. The hired mourners were near the foot of the bier.

At the appointed hour a coffin was brought and the body placed within it, the top screwed on, and immediately the body was borne to the graveyard. The procession moved through the streets with little or no regularity. Their course was more zig-zag than straight, for they say the spirit of the dead man abhors the grave, and this course indicates his unwillingness to be buried.

Sometimes the procession moves frantically in jerks and starts, going backward, sidewise, and in every imaginable way revealing the reluctance of the corpse to be interred. There is music from drums, horns, accordions, and whatever else will make melody or noise. At the grave the body is deposited with a short, weird ceremony by the master of ceremonies, after which the people return to the town and prepare for the "big play" which follows the demise of every important man.

After a few days a division of the dead man's property is made. The heads of the wives are shaven, and they wash themselves in a stream of water. If near the ocean, they dip therein. They then become the property of the next man in the family, who keeps them or distributes them among other relatives, according to his judgment or will. The women have no choice in the matter. They generally obey, going where they are sent.

DEATH AND MOURNING

The saddest features of native life are apparent during severe sickness and death. If the remedies employed should fail to effect a speedy cure, superstition seeks a cause of the illness in witchcraft, and many succumb to this.

Friends approach a sick or dying man, putting such questions as: "Have you bewitched any one?" "Are you a witch?" Or sometimes the heathen doctor will imperatively say, "You are a witch, and unless you acknowledge your sorceries I will not be able to cure you." The deluded creature, for the sake of a fancied cure, will acknowledge having committed sorceries when he knows it to be false, saying: "I must have done it. My spirit at night, while I slept, wandered from my body and committed the deed."

Death causes loud and great mourning; the air is rent with lamentations and heart-breaking cries. All the inhabitants of a native village are expected to mourn at the death of one of the conspicuous of their number, and friends from other places come in to join the mourners.

FOLK-LORE FROM AFRICA

All the virtues of the deceased are rehearsed in weird, chanting strains by some woman who leads in a sort of recitative, the rest joining in the voluble refrain. No one can look upon such scenes without being affected, feeling deeply how utterly desolate heathenism is and how forlorn is mankind without Jesus Christ, who declares Himself to be "the resurrection and the life."

Graves are very shallow, usually three feet deep at most. Often they are too short. We have heard of instances when persons of extra weight have stepped upon the stomach of the corpse to force it down in the grave, where it lay in a cramped and curved position. The body of an ordinary native is wrapped in a mat made of grass as a shroud, while honored dead are swathed in many cloths of gaudy colors and given all the attention that belongs to their rank.

In some instances women may not attend the corpse to the grave, because Nor, the country devil, is shouting vociferously while the body is being interred. As an embalming process recourse is taken to smoke, sometimes, which leaves the body a mass of cured flesh. A disgusting practice is that of keeping the body above ground until decomposition sets in, making it unsightly and unapproachable to all but the misguided heathen; another is exhuming the putrid remains where they have lain for a short while in what is known as "half ground"

MISSIONARY STORY SKETCHES

—that is, half buried, covered up in the grave without the usual ceremonies, until all arrangements are made in the final settlement and disposition of the deceased's estate.

Then a big play is given to the honor and in the memory of the dead. The corpse, with its falling, decaying flesh, is dressed and propped up on a stool, and around it gather its devoted fanatical admirers to pay their final tribute ere it is laid deeper in the earth, to remain. While this goes on there is a salute of guns, drinking of intoxicating beverages, and feasting, music, and dancing. Presents are bestowed, and sympathy is extended to the bereaved.

NATIVE INCIDENTS AND ITEMS FROM RELIGIOUS LIFE

DIFFICULTIES IN PRESENTING THE GOSPEL

Missionaries in Liberia employ the English language and literature in their evangelistic and educational work among the various tribes. This method is almost general, and while convenient for the missionaries who are English-speaking, it rather handicaps the natives, to whom the gospel as preached in English is often an unmeaning tale.

The poverty of the native dialects makes it impossible to convey to the heathen mind many of the ideas and words found in our religious and secular books. This is especially true with abstract truth. Interpreters whose education is liberal supply the deficiency with gestures, paraphrases, parables, etc. But at best the raw natives get only a faint and inadequate conception of the truth. Only that truth which is stripped of all superfluities can with any degree of appreciation be grasped. Anything else is but a waste of time and energy.

MISSIONARY STORY SKETCHES

For, though interpreters who are employed help matters a little, generally their knowledge of English is limited, and they often fail in grasping the meaning of an idea and are therefore unable to convey it to the people.

The missionary who in preaching to a native audience took for his text Revelations iii, 3, "I will come on thee as a thief in the night, and thou shalt not know what hour I shall come upon thee," was very much embarrassed by the interpreter's odd way of putting the text. He said that Jesus Christ was a thief and would come as such. This, of course, was not welcome news to the audience.

The disorder and uproar that followed would have broken up the meeting but for a timely correction that translated the text properly and presented it in its true light.

Discoursing on the Holy Sacrament and afterwards patiently catechizing a class of converts in the rudiments of the doctrine, a missionary proceeded to administer the Communion. He had striven to elucidate all difficulties touching the nature and end of the Lord's Supper, and felt quite sure that he had succeeded; but the interpreter, in translating those sentences in the ritual which accompany the partaking of the bread, namely: "The body of our Lord Jesus Christ which was given for thee," etc., emphasized the fact that the bread was the *body* of our Lord. This greatly astonished the chief of the district, who was present and also a communicant. He interrupted the service with a sudden outburst, and, calling the missionary by name, exclaimed, "You lie; I myself been see your woman make dem bread!"

To the untutored African in a native gathering there was nothing either rude or sacrilegious in the remark.

The missionary attempted an explanation, but he said himself that his explanation was never satisfactory until he had mastered the intricacies of the native dialects.

CONTROVERSIAL DOCTRINE AMONG THE HEATHEN

Very often denominational differences between professed Christians prove perplexing to the heathen and greatly retard missionary work among them.

The following incident occurred in a Liberian town some years ago:

A band of touring missionaries representing two different Churches entered the town and began zealously to labor for their respective denominations. The one who first gained audience with the king proceeded to point out to him and his people the way of salvation.

MISSIONARY STORY SKETCHES

Fearing lest the missionaries of the other Church would make headway in inculcating doctrinal truth among the people, he felt it his bounden duty to forestall his brethren of the sister Church by discoursing on the doctrine of baptism himself at his first opportunity.

Therefore he presented a comprehensive discourse on the doctrine of baptism, defending the mode as adopted by his Church with unusual earnestness and with a scholarship worthy of a professor's chair. Having to speak through an interpreter, and the discourse being somewhat lengthy, his hearers were wearied by it.

However, just before closing he succeeded in gaining the attention of his drowsy listeners by making a long pause, and then calling aloud the king by name, saying that unless he and his subjects believed in the Lord Jesus Christ and were baptized in the mode he had advocated, sprinkling or pouring the water, they would not enter the kingdom of heaven.

Of course, questions of doctrine were all new to the pagan king and his people. They were open to accept almost any statement coming from the "God man." So they decided that the missionary knew what he was talking about and were becoming settled in their minds that there was no alternative to what they had just heard.

FOLK-LORE FROM AFRICA

But on the next Sabbath the other Church was before the same king and people. Their leader discussed the same doctrine they had listened to on the previous Sabbath, but, of course, putting the emphasis upon immersion. He declared that it was the right and only mode of baptism, and that unless the king and his tribe were baptized in that way they could not be regarded worthy of the Church below nor above.

The gray-haired king, shifting nervously about in his seat, recognized at once the dilemma in which he was placed by the preachers of these different denominations, and, standing up in the course of the sermon, demanded of the preacher whose word he must keep.

"You say I must be immersed, and any other way than this is no baptism at all. The other man says I must be sprinkled or poured, and that his way is the only right way," he said. "Well," continued he, "since you God people disagree, I will keep my devil way, for we devil people never differ from one another."

Thus having decidedly spoken, he and his people retired from the room, leaving both preachers and the conflicting doctrines they preached alone, with a feeling that in this instance paganism had trimphed over Christianity.

MISSIONARY STORY SKETCHES

TIRED OF WAITING

A missionary was discoursing on the doctrine of the new birth before a native audience, and closed with an appeal that the unsaved of his congregation surrender to Christ, that He might give them a new heart.

An impatient native chief, who said he desired a new heart and who had made a brief trial in quest of it, but who was very anxious concerning the issues of a palaver which was going on in one of his half towns, went forward and said to the missionary, "When is God coming to give me a new heart and save me?"

In reply to the answer to his question he said, "I am tired of waiting for Him."

And thus speaking, he got up and strode nervously from the room.

THE ATTITUDE OF MOHAMMEDANISM IN WEST AFRICA

An expedition to Kano was undertaken some years ago in the interest of commerce and missions by an eminent bishop of West Africa. Kano is a great commercial emporium in the Central Soudan, and the bishop contemplated the establishment of a medical mission there, and an educational work later on. It was his belief that if at this strategic point, with its vast population and resources, European civilization could be brought in contact with the natives, wonderful religious and commercial results would soon follow.

Kano has a resident population estimated at about one million. It has extensive commercial connection with regions further inland, touching Lake Chad, Khartoum, and Tripoli.

Proceeding from Lagos and traveling through the Yoruba country, a distance of two hundred and fifty miles, the bishop and his party reached Jebba, and from there traveled northward to Kano. The journey from Jebba to Kano required six weeks, traveling ten miles a day on foot.

The reception given the party while at Kano shows the attitude of a Mohammedan king toward Christian missions.

While receiving the party in a magnificent room, the king scarcely condescended to greet them with the usual heartiness characteristic of the African. Turning to the interpreter with manifest anger, he asked, "What do those men want in this country?"

He was told the object of their errand; but, although every effort was made by the party to persuade the king, by earnest entreaties and appeals, to accept Christian teachers, they were met by a cold rebuff.

MISSIONARY STORY SKETCHES

"There is no need of Christian teachers in my country," he said. "We have enough of our own. Not even did we need medical missions. The Koran is all-sufficient and is an excellent substitute for medicines for my people. They need nothing from the outside world."

With this the king ordered the party to leave his city. The subjects of His Majesty shouted cries of approval to his words. He was proclaimed a lion, and they cried, "May God give you long life!"

SHIPWRECK TO FAITH [1]

There is a certain man of the Kroo tribe, living in Krootown, who, several years ago, from all outward manifestation, was a sincere adherent to a certain Church and was regular in his attendance at all of its services. He contributed small sums for the support of the Church and was strict in his observance of the Sabbath. He refrained from gambling and drinking liquor, and all things of a similar nature, although he was surrounded by many who did them.

"The Lord is my Shepherd; I shall not want;" "Blessed are the meek, for they shall inherit the kingdom of earth;" "Seek ye first the kingdom of God, and all these things shall be added unto

---

[1] From "Liberia and West Africa."

you," and similar passages of Scripture had been interpreted literally by this man. He had concluded that if he served God, who was the giver of all things, he would prosper more than those who did not, and so he served with that end in view. He gave the "God palaver," as he thought, a fair trial, but he had more trouble than his neighbors, who made no profession. He began to despair of any return for his diligent service, and decided that he would resume his former manner of life and enjoy perhaps his former prosperity.

One Sunday morning, when his teacher and pastor passed his house on the way to service, he saw to his great surprise this man beating dumboy[2] vigorously, a thing which he would not do formerly. He was gently reprimanded for his breach of the Sabbath day and asked if he did not know that was wrong.

"You see," he replied, with somewhat of a wild stare after he had been remonstrated with, "I don't sabey dis 'God palaver.' All dis people he drink liquor, he gamble, he kill fish Sunday, and all dem ting. He got plenty chop. He woman born pickaninny, dem pickaninny lib. I pray.

---

[2] Preparing cassava for food is known as beating *dumboy*. Cassava is an esculent root that grows plentifully in Liberia. It is a common diet. One of the ways of preparing it is by beating it to a pulp in a wooden mortar with a pestle. It is served with hot soup, highly seasoned with pepper and palm oil. Fish and beef are also added to the soup. It is correctly eaten by swallowing without masticating.

I sing. I serve God good. God poke fun at me. My woman born pickaninny, all two dem pickaninny done die. My goat born pickaninny, dem pickaninny he done die too. My house up river burn down. My farm spile. What I go do now? God poke fun at me."

His pastor made a serious effort to reason with him, and to explain that his service was not to be rewarded in this life, perhaps, but in the life to come. But he would hear none of it, and threw up his hands in wild confusion and said, "No, no, no, no; I go do dis ting."

And the man who had spent so much time in trying to instruct and direct him went away with a heavy heart, an earnest prayer on his lips.

"GONGLA"—A RASCAL

An independent missionary, who gave a number of years of splendid service in Africa, gives an interesting experience of how he dealt with an offender. It was his belief that missionaries should not employ force or threats, or, for that matter, even take recourse to the law of the land in dealing with offenders. He says that while in one or two instances he felt it necessary to do this, yet each time his conscience troubled him afterward. He counsels that we follow the injunction given in Hebrews, "Taking joyously the spoiling of our goods," leaving the matter of avenging the wrong in the hands of God.

After he had been in a certain locality for a number of years he met a native whose nickname was Gongla, which, being interpreted, means "rascal." And the missionary felt that he was not misnamed, for Gongla seemed thoroughly bad and was the worst native he had ever met. He employed the time in gambling; he was very quarrelsome; he was hard-hearted and dishonest. And yet the missionary says that God made it very plain to him that he lacked in love for this unfortunate creature. So he made Gongla a subject of prayer. He went out of his way to treat him kindly, so as to win him, but found him almost an impossible man to deal with. Soon Gongla was quarreling with him.

One Sabbath, when the missionary and his boys went to a neighboring town to conduct religious services, Gongla, who had been lurking about the place, broke into the mission house and, entering a trunk which was locked, stole all the missionary possessed in money, which was about twenty-five dollars, as well as some valuable papers. It seemed that the quarrel had hardened him to commit this act. The missionary had no evidence that Gongla had committed the theft, but was quite confident that it was he. He, however, requested his boys to maintain silence concerning the matter until sufficient evidence could be obtained.

Before long Gongla became reckless and bought a large quantity of dry goods, and the missionary's suspicions were then confirmed. He sent for him and reasoned with him, urging him to make a confession and restitution of the goods, promising him forgiveness; but the native angrily dared the missionary to prosecute him. A warrant was made for his arrest, but he escaped and became a fugitive for two years.

At the end of that time he returned, but kept furtively out of the way, dodging about in the forest and bush. Finally this exposure, and probably the nervous strain of his fear, cost him his health, and news came to the missionary, to his great surprise, that Gongla was dying.

"Now," thought he, "this is my opportunity to try to lead him to repentance." And hastening to Gongla, he found him lying upon a wretched and filthy bed of mat. He knelt by the side of this unfortunate man and prayed that ere the soul departed from the diseased body it at least would be freed from the disease of sin, being made whole by repentance and acceptance of the Divine Healer.

And his prayer was not in vain, for the heart of Gongla was moved, and he confessed his crime. Gently the missionary pointed the dying man to Christ, and earnestly he talked with him. And before nightfall he knew that there was joy in heaven over one more soul that was saved, as waiting angels bore the redeemed spirit upward on their wings of light.

"GOD MOVES IN A MYSTERIOUS WAY"

Visiting an interior town, the same missionary was making arrangements for the building of a mission house. He was entertained successively at the different homes, and on the last night the house assigned him as a stopping place he was in but a short while, as the owner of it came late in the evening to take possession, and he was given another for the evening.

Arrived in his new quarters, he shifted his portable cot in his room, seeking a convenient place, and finally decided upon placing it in a position from which he could command a view from the window. A small incident the placing of his cot would seem, but it was foreordained to work a mighty end.

A fire was made in the center of the room, and, the smoke rising from it in all parts of the room being disagreeable, the missionary opened the window so as to allow it to escape, and retired for the night with it thus open. At midnight he awoke with a start, and, looking out of the window, he saw a house ablaze. It was the king's storeroom.

Rushing out in his sleeping apparel, he yelled at the top of his voice, "Fire! Fire!" This was a strange cry to the people, and some of them in the town thought it an alarm of war, for they had heard these words spoken by the Americo-Liberian soldiers in battle. Water was brought and thrown upon the burning building, and the fire was soon extinguished.

A moment more and it would have been too late to prevent an awful explosion, as among the things in the attic of the structure were great quantities of powder placed there by the king. These were already hot when the fire was conquered.

In a few hours the town was quiet again, and the missionary returned to his room, destined to become on the morrow the recipient of the whole-hearted gratitude of these people and a welcome messenger in their midst. He threw himself again upon his cot and pondered on the happenings. Clearly in them he saw the workings of a Divine Providence, who had chosen him to be His instrument and who thus paved the way for him to enter the people's hearts and establish a mission to lead them to Christianity. And he knew that for this purpose he had placed his cot by the window; for this purpose he had awakened to behold the fire, when none other saw it; and he knew that

FOLK-LORE FROM AFRICA

the fire was but another element God had chosen to fulfill His plan for the redemption of this pagan village, which was rendered receptive of the gospel truths by the happenings of this night, when the missionary played the part of a hero.

AN AFRICAN'S WELCOME

Our first experience with the natives on reaching Liberia is interesting, in that it reveals their sense of appreciation for the help that they expect us to give. After the service they crowded around us to shake hands and express themselves. One, speaking for the congregation, said, "Daddy, you done come from big 'Merikay to teach we dem God palaver?"

"Yes," said I.

"Mammy, he done come for dem same ting?"

"Yes, both of us have come from America to help you and all who need our aid."

"We be too glad plenty, daddy; you done come, mammy done come, all two come, help poor we. Daddy, it be fine! We heart live for lay down. You come teach we white man book; den we know too much sense, and learn plenty 'Merikay ways, and live pray God proper bom by."

While the "witch doctors," "the ju-jus," the Gri-Gri Bush, are still believed by many, and the devil worshiped and "dashed" and heathenism practiced, yet the gospel and Christian education are gradually and surely doing their purifying work among many of Africa's untutored children. It is filtering in its higher and better New Testament ideas of purity and life, transforming this crude and perverted humanity into a noble type of an enlightened Christian character.

GOD A PRESENT HELP IN TROUBLE

By order of the Supreme Court of Liberia, Fahn Saco, a native of the Pessey tribe, who was under conviction for murder in the lower court, was discharged. It was made clear by his attorney that he killed his assistant in self-defense.

The case from the beginning attracted wide attention, and it was thought by many that he would swing upon the gallows for the expiation of his crime; but upon careful and impartial investigation the decision was reached giving him his liberation from prison and his release from the hangman's rope.

The interest which the decision created was intense, and the event produced a scene which an onlooker could not soon forget.

Fahn Saco was a man of powerful build, tall, and stalwart. His country cloth thrown loosely around his athletic frame exposed his breast and limbs and gave him the appearance of a bronze statue as he stood up to receive his discharge from the jailer.

For several months his fate had hung in the balance, and he had hovered between doubt and fear. When the news reached him in his cell that he was set at liberty by the court, he walked toward the center of the prison, his step firm and his port lordly. But as he stood thus for some moments, in his eyes tears gathered and his frame trembled with emotion.

With quivering lips and faltering words he thanked the judge and all who had aided in his release; but when asked whom he thanked the most, he lifted his eyes heavenward, saying, in his native tongue, "God."

Thus this poor heathen in his distress realized with the psalmist of old that "God is our refuge and strength, an ever-present help in trouble."

QUÆ AND HIS HEATHEN MOTHER

When a little boy named Quæ had been in the mission home for two years, one day a crowd of his people from the interior came to see him. He did not recognize any of them, as he had been too young—not more than three years old—when brought to the mission. And having become accustomed to seeing those about him clothed, he hesitated to make friends with the scantily-clad visitors.

Seats were offered the party, which were accepted by the men, the women preferring to sit on the floor, as in their country it is usual for the men to occupy the stool or bench, while the women squat on the hard, beaten floor.

The missionary sat just in front of the eldest woman in the crowd, and Quæ nestled down beside her, covering himself with the folds of her dress. The interpreter of the party, whose name was Jolly-marly, then said that when Quæ's people had the big war, three years before, in their country, many of them were separated from their children and had lost them; and further, that the woman sitting in front of the missionary was the mother of the little boy at her side.

The missionary's heart gave a great leap, for she feared to lose Quæ, the favorite and baby of the family. However, she spoke to Quæ and told him that Parmah was his mother, and that he must speak to her. The child drew back in horror and surprise.

"O no!" he cried. "I don't know her, and I don't want to go to her."

"That is your *y ay y ay*" (mother), said the missionary. "Can't you speak to her?"

"I don't know her," again repeated the child.

After a little gentle persuasion, accompanied by a caress, Quæ, grasping the missionary's dress and drawing her forward with him, timidly said in his native tongue, "How do, woman?"

The poor woman was delighted, and she lifted up her bare arms (for her clothing consisted only of a loin cloth, leaving the upper portion of her body uncovered) and said: "Come here, baby. Come to your mother."

He finally allowed her to take him in her arms, at the same time keeping a firm hold on the missionary's skirt. The poor woman patted him gently all over, from head to foot. Tears of joy streamed down her wrinkled face as she held her only child, whom she had mourned as lost.

The missionary, sitting down in front of her on a chair, ruminated that, after all, a mother is a mother, whether civilized or heathen. The woman's arms still encircled her little one. She moved herself along the floor until she could reach the missionary's feet, one of which she held tight with both hands and laid her cheeks against it, and with tears streaming from her eyes spoke as from the depths of her soul: "Thank you, mammy; thank you. This is my only child, and I have made myself sick crying for him. Now that I find him, I am happy. Keep him as your own boy, and teach him book and 'God palaver.'"

MISSIONARY STORY SKETCHES

WHAT IS THE GREATEST THING IN THE WORLD?

This question was put to a class of native boys in one of our missions at Cape Palmas, and these were their respective answers:

Douah said that the Bible is, because the Bible tells us how God loves us, and it saves and feeds our soul.

Dapo said that wisdom is, because it gives us sense to make things, and it gives us sense to govern the nations well.

Walla said that the Holy Ghost is, because He teaches us to do the will of God, and makes us understand the Word of God, and gives us strength to do His will.

Donnah said that to preach the gospel is, because it tells the people about God.

After a few moments' talk we all agreed that "love" is the greatest thing in the world, because "God is love."

TRAINING-SCHOOL FOR "DEVIL DOCTORS"

"Devil doctors," or medicine men, as they are sometimes called, are to be found in nearly all the West African tribes. Young men who choose the profession first seek their instructors and ascertain whether they will be acceptable candidates or not. When they are ready to start for the "devil doctors'" quarters they must supply themselves with a piece of white cloth, a bowl, and a spoon for their own use. They are not allowed to eat of everything in common with the others, but only of such things as are permissible according to the laws of the native institution, and out of their own vessels. They must not eat fish from the creeks and streams.

When they reach the "devil bush" they are received by the one in charge and given an apron of bamboo fibers to put on, a monkey skin to sit upon, bangles for the ankles, and a piece of medicine cloth to fasten upon each arm and leg. A white substance like chalk is given them to chew. The face and body is anointed with this chalk every morning, and circles made around their eyes with it, which gives the body a hideous appearance. The bath must be taken late at night, when no one is near.

During the first six months the hair is not cut, and the cutting of it at the expiration of this period constitutes an event of moment in "devil doctor's" circle. It commemorates a sort of milestone in their training. A chicken is then killed, its head hidden, and the apprentices asked to find it. Their success and the quickness with which they discover it counts for aptitude and scholarship. The finder is congratulated and cheered by those present.

During the next six months they are specially trained along the line of medicines. Their teaching embraces instructions in those things which kill as well as those which cure. They become experts in poisoning. When they have mastered all that is taught, the making of charms and fetiches included, their friends are invited to come for the final test.

This time a dog is killed, its head hidden, and the young "devil doctors" told to find it. Should they succeed, their heads are again shaven. They take off the bamboo apron, put on their cloth, receive the congratulations of friends and are ready to launch out upon the practice of their profession among the people. They are styled "doctors" and are leaders in the native community. They are generally very clever fellows.

CONVERSION OF A "DEVIL DOCTOR"

"Devil doctors," as described in the foregoing, are the men who keep the people tied down, as it were, with a galling chain of ignorance, superstition, and witchcraft. They conceive plans to keep the poor natives constantly in the darkness and in dread of impending dangers. For these reasons the

FOLK-LORE FROM AFRICA

"devil doctors" require large "dashes" from different families to avert approaching catastrophes, bring children to the family, and keep off death by ferocious beasts. They make charms and ju-jus, which these poor misled heathen wear, and in which they have implicit faith.

Once two of our native Christians went out to visit a far-distant town, and as is the custom in Africa, they slept in the town, where night overtook them, which, on the evening of our story, was in Beabo. After supper they called the people, as many as would come, to hear "God palaver." Many gathered, instigated by curiosity, and among them was the "devil doctor" of the whole tribe, who happened to be in that town at this particular time, working his charms and making ju-jus.

This old agent of Satan was known to be a bitter foe to missionary enterprise. His presence was a surprise to these Christians, but they continued singing and praying and talking to the people in their own tongue of the "power of God unto salvation." The meeting closed in due time, and early next morning, before they were out of their hammocks, they saw this old "devil doctor" coming and expected a bitter contest.

However, to their surprise, he said that he had come to bid them good morning and ask a further explanation of the words spoken the night before. "For," said he, "to me it sounds sweet, and I am going to give up 'devil way' and try to do 'God way.'"

Continuing, he said that in his sleep he had had a vision. He saw himself at the fork of two paths, one leading in the big bush and the other in the clearings among the native Christians. The light shone along the path of the latter, while the other path was dark. The dream had disturbed him greatly.

The native workers were for a moment so surprised at this unexpected development that they were almost speechless. They told him that salvation was very near to him; that all he had to do was believe in the Lord Jesus Christ and be saved. He said he was ready to do this, and as an evidence he was willing to eat crawfish before them and the people, thus signifying that he broke his charm and became a follower of Christ.

"I have been deceiving the people for years," he said, "making them believe that there is power in the charms and ju-jus I have been making for them. My business in the town at this time was to make the tribal fetich, which was to protect the people from war and bring male children."

But after his peace with God he exclaimed, "I live to pray God. I make no more ju-ju now." He begged them piteously to help him to pray, for he had been a great sinner.

FOLK-LORE FROM AFRICA

This was the opening wedge for Christianity in this town, and since then many have accepted Christ. Idolatry and witchcraft must give way to the Prince of Peace.

JASPER GRANT'S DECISION

Jasper Grant, a convert from heathenism and a successful native worker of long standing in the Methodist Mission at Cape Palmas, suffered many annoyances and persecutions from his fellow tribesmen when he united with the Church and broke away completely from the old beliefs in which he was brought up.

For this he was beaten with many stripes, and such was the hostility toward him from the natives about him on account of this radical change of faith that his life was threatened again and again, and the missionary in charge of the station where he labored feared lest he would be killed outright.

The missionary submitted the case to Bishop Taylor for advice. The bishop, after carefully investigating the matter, advised that Jasper Grant be placed on his own responsibility and decide his case for himself. When this was told Jasper, his prompt reply to the bishop, which reveals something of his sturdy manhood and devotion to his Master, was as follows:

MISSIONARY STORY SKETCHES

"I was born here; these people who want to kill me are my people; they have the same hatred toward Christ and Christians that I had before I found Jesus; so I have no quarrel with them. I patiently bear their unmerciful thrashings, and if the Lord wants me to die for His cause, I prefer to die on my own native soil."

Jasper's decision soon became known throughout his section, and his persecution gradually ceased as his countrymen saw further evidences of his stability and unshrinking devotion to the cause he loved dearer than life.

Jasper proved to be of the material from which heroes are made. His people who formerly dared to take his life, latterly recognized his firmness and bravery, and such was their admiration and respect for him that they sang his name in their country's war songs, along with others who had distinguished themselves for valor in battle.

But greater than this is his loyalty to Christ and his devoted constancy in the Christian faith and his self-sacrificing labors for his people. Jasper's prompt decision was the pivotal point of his life.

May there be many others like him to rise up in the midst of heathenism and shine forth as lights amid the darkness!

FOLK-LORE FROM AFRICA

THE KING OF KINGS' FAMILY

There was organized several years ago by Jasper Grant, a native Christian in charge of the Plebe Station, on the Cape Palmas District, an organization known as the King of Kings' Family. Its purpose is for mutual help and protection against the forces of heathenism. The constitution of the organization is as follows:

"We, the undersigned, members of the Methodist Episcopal Mission, do hereby agree, God being our helper, to stand by each other in any trouble that may arise.

"From this day forward we will have nothing to do with our heathen families in regard to securing help from them. And because we ask nothing of them they can not have anything to do or say in reference to us and our families.

"We are one family in God. When He sees fit to take one of us from this world, the remaining numbers will care for his or her family.

"We will have nothing to do with spirituous liquors, including palm wine, bamboo wine, and tobacco."

All members are requested to keep strictly the last clause of this constitution, not only by not using these things themselves, but also by in no way assisting others to obtain them.

They also require all of their members to

carefully keep the Sabbath, especially in regard to watching rice birds on Sunday.

The society was organized because the native Christians felt sorely the need of some power to offset the heathen customs to which they were often subjected. Should a man die, his wife and children belonged to his people, and they could claim them and force them back into heathenism. Children who have been in the mission stations for years have been taken out and given to the heathen family. Protestations were of no avail. The King of Kings' Family is an effort to meet this problem.

A LETTER FROM A CHRISTIAN MANDINGO

Among the many tribes inhabiting the vast hinterlands of Liberia, the Mandingoes are by no means the least interesting. They dwell in the Mandingo country, which lies in the northeastern part of Liberia, beyond the Pessey country. Musardu was for many years the capital of the Western Mandingoes. It was visited by Mr. Benjamin Anderson, a Liberian explorer, in 1868. In a book entitled "A Journey to Musardu" he gives a most interesting description of the country and its inhabitants. The Mandingoes are much further advanced than any of the pagan tribes in

Liberia. They have an extensive commerce, which extends to the northeast as far as Timbuctoo. Gold and other minerals are found there. Cattle, including horses, are bred in large numbers, and dense forest lands yield to grassy plains and park lands.

The Mandingoes are devout followers of Mohammed. They read the Koran, build schools for instruction, and mosques as places of prayer; they are in direct communication with Mecca, to which pilgrimages are constantly made. They are aggressive propagandists of Mohammedanism. We have heard of whole towns and districts in the Western Soudan embracing Islam through her zealous and irrepressible advocates.

There are in Freetown, Sierra Leone, to the northeast of Liberia, several mosques, with a Mohammedan population of five thousand. The Mohammedan tribes represented in the city are Foulah's, Mandingoes, Susus, Limbas, Timinis, Sarakulais, and Akus. On the first of January the Mohammedans hold their great festival celebrating the revelation of the Koran to Mohammed.

Mohammedanism is rapidly spreading over Western Africa and is pressing down into Liberia. More pagans are being Mohammedanized in Liberia than Christianized. The yearly accessions to Christianity from the Mandingoes may be counted, as it were, on the fingers. There are no

MISSIONARY STORY SKETCHES

Christian missions in the Mandingo country. The few converts to Christianity from this tribe are those living near to Liberian settlements.

The interesting letter which we subjoin is from the Rev. Dauda Kana, a Mandingo convert of Christianity. He was at the time of its writing a teacher in Rick's Institute, a Baptist institution in Liberia.

The American Bible Society placed in the hands of Bishop Hartzell, several years ago, some copies of the Holy Bible in the Arabic language. One of the Bibles was presented to Rick's Institute, to be used in the chapel services when Kana conducted them. He read passages from the book first in Arabic, and then translated them into English. Another copy was given to Kana personally. After receiving the book he addressed a letter to Bishop Hartzell, written in legible and beautiful Arabic, of which the following is a translation:

"In the name of the Gracious, the Merciful! Praise be to God, who has brought us together in love. He alone is God, who sent messengers before He Himself came.

"My brother, may God bless you! The present that you have given to me is in the name of Christ, that it may be used for Him. The Lord will bless you. What you have done is a witness of the love of God in your heart.

"Our God is your God. May the peace of God rest upon you! You are sent as a messenger

FOLK-LORE FROM AFRICA

to the house of the Lord, and whoever accepts of the Christ, the peace of the Lord will rest upon them. May God make you a watchman in deed and in truth! Amen.   DAUDA KANA."

VISITING NATIVE CHIEFS

African chiefs are usually interesting to visit, especially when no suspicions are attached to the visit and it is known that the visitor is a representative character, having authority, and one coming in the discharge of professional duty.

Rev. C. A. Pitman, of the Liberia Conference, in an official visit to Bopora, made at the request of Bishop Gilbert Haven, tells of the reception given him by Mo-Moru, the ruler of Bopora. He describes him as a man six feet six inches tall, with a white beard, an object of special admiration to his people.

Bopora at that time had a population of fifteen thousand. It is a barricaded town situated in a valley with a chain of mountains on all sides stretching in the distance. The scenery is beautiful and of grandeur. As capital of the Boatswain or Condoes, it has figured prominently in the history of Liberia, and has been a center of stirring scenes in native life.

Mo-moru had, near the town, his famous catfish pool. The fishes were his pets, and his favorite pastime was to feed them regularly. He regarded them as gods and protectors of his kingdom, bestowing upon him wealth and prosperity. A penalty was attached for interfering with them. They measured from one to three feet in length and were sharklike in their disposition, feeding at times upon the carcasses of murdered slaves and captives in war.

Mo-moru received the missionary with characteristic heartiness and with a hospitality becoming to African royalty. He presented to his guest a large sheep.

When the object of the mission was stated the chief said that he was well pleased to have a visit from one who had come so far to see him, and that he was glad his purpose was to assist him in the work of teaching his people.

In speaking of the children, Mr. Pitman said that in the Mohammedan school at Bopora they were taught to worship catfish as gods. As he and his companions passed through the town the little boys followed them foot to foot, wherever they went, even crowding upon them in the hut upon their beds. They sat upon their laps despite the remonstrances of their parents. When they left Bopora the children wept and entreated them to remain.

At To-to-Kollie, another populous town, the king, Benga Kollie, was absent when Mr. Pitman

FOLK-LORE FROM AFRICA

arrived, but soon returned with a suite of ten armed men and five boys. He extended a cordial reception to the strangers and presented his compliments with the gift of a fine goat, which was killed and served for dinner.

King Benga Kollie was affable and pleasant, saying that if the school was established in his country he would attend it himself. When told that he could learn, being a young man, he said, "Yes, my heart is willing."

Before leaving To-to-Kollie the king gave further assurances of his willingness to encourage mission work in his midst, by signing a written agreement to which were attached names of witnesses.

The following, from a letter sent to the writer by Bishop Hartzell, records his experience with a paramount chief in East Africa:

"Recently I visited the kraal or town of Umtassa, where lives the paramount chief of this whole region. He received me in state with his counselors about him. I spoke to an educated Zulu, and he to Masboua, and he to the chief interpreter, and what the chief said was transmitted to me through the same channel.

"The second language prevented any 'bad spirit' accompanying my words. I took him a blanket for a present; but it required a long palaver before he would consent to take it, as he had nothing to give in return, he claimed. He said the spirit would do him harm if he took it without some return. I said the Spirit I worshiped taught to give without expecting anything in return. Finally he compromised in a cup of water from a spring near by, which he gave me with great ceremony after taking a sip himself."

THE OUTSTRETCHED HANDS OF ETHIOPIA

At a Conference session held at Clay Ashland in 1901 a large number of native helpers were present and reported their work. The Bassa, Mendi, Golah, Kroo, Pesseh, and Grebo tribes were represented. A praise service in these several native tongues and in English was held. "Come to Jesus" and other familiar hymns were sung. The effect of this mingling of voices and languages in the worship of God was wonderfully inspiring. The Holy Spirit graciously manifested His presence and power among all present. The outlook for our native work never seemed brighter. The natives were eager for the gospel, and on every hand were making loud calls for Christian teachers and preachers to come among them.

The following letter, written by a young man of the Grebo tribe for the king and chiefs of Half

FOLK-LORE FROM AFRICA

Cavalla, an important section of Southern Liberia, is a proof of this. The petition was as a wailing cry from heathenism for help and gospel light. The outstretched hands of Ethiopia need to be filled with the blessings of the gospel of Jesus Christ:

HALF CAVALLA, LIBERIA,
January, 1901.

To Bishop Hartzell and Liberia Methodist Conference, to meet in Clay Ashland, March 5, 1901:

We, the king and chiefs of Half Cavalla, do need the doctrine of yours to be taught to ourselves and children. We need the school to be opened here, and also the church to be built. Your doctrine is always being heard and read by our children. It is a pure and powerful way which leads to eternal life. So fail not to open with us. We can not stop you from enlightening our native country, no one to stop you but the government, whom we know will stop nobody from doing good.

We are tired of revolting; looking to God for help. Yours truly,

KING HNE,	CHIEF NANO BOA,
CHIEF DADE,	CHIEF NANO GREBO,
CHIEF SEBO,	CHIEF BLIO KPADA,
CHIEF KODADO-BUO,	CHIEF TAGU GEDEE.
CHIEF MADO BOA,	

MISSIONARY STORY SKETCHES

"THOU SHALT FIND IT AFTER MANY DAYS"

Years ago one of our missionaries under Bishop Taylor became interested in a little native boy living in Cape Palmas, Liberia. After leading him to Christ and giving him a fair elementary education in the mission school which she taught, she sent him to the Basle Mission, an industrial school farther south on the African coast.

The missionary afterwards returned to the United States to recruit her shattered health. This boy in the meanwhile applied himself diligently to the work she selected for him. After mastering his trade he returned to his people a skilled mechanic, capable of doing the work of a carpenter, cabinet maker, and upholsterer. We have seen specimens of his work, and they bear marks of superior workmanship.

If this faithful missionary did nothing else than to give this boy his start in life and put him in the path of usefulness and industry, she wrought nobly and well. Many such fruits of the self-sacrificing labors of American missionaries lie scattered here and there on the African continent. It is impossible to estimate the far-reaching good such labors yield in the spread of practical Christianity and the development of character.

In the establishment of our industrial missions

FOLK-LORE FROM AFRICA

we recognize this fact and anticipate these ends. Christianity and civilization should go hand in hand. It is not enough to do evangelistic work alone—important as it is—nor yet to deal theoretically in text books; but, as a complement to these, there should be thorough training in industrial pursuits to fit the youth for practical life. There must be industries to prevent idleness, for idleness not only leads to poverty, but to moral and physical degeneracy.

The fact that the importance of industrial education is widely admitted and that it is steadily growing, especially in connection with mission work, attests its value and utility. This kind of work ought to be encouraged and generally supported, for the case of this African boy illustrates the force of the words of Scripture, "Cast thy bread upon the waters; for thou shalt find it after many days."

WHY A NATIVE MAN OBJECTED TO CHRISTIANITY

1. Because God gave white man book, and gave black man ju-ju, or fetich, to keep him.

2. Because we can't see God, but we can see ju-ju and talk it.

MISSIONARY STORY SKETCHES

A NATIVE CHRISTIAN LAD'S TESTIMONY IN THE CLASS-MEETING

I love God, for He is a good spirit. I hate the devil, for he is a bad spirit. If I mind the devil I can't get one banana to eat. If I mind God, I will set down in a good place forever. Amen.

SPECIMEN LETTERS FROM NATIVE CHRISTIANS, ADDRESSED TO BISHOP HARTZELL IN 1900

DEAR BISHOP: How glad I will be to see you! I am very sorry to see the mission here broken up. I pray God you may take up this station again. I hope you may come up here next year, if possible, to see the place. I would like to talk with you about the mission. I and my people are willing to give, by the help of God, to have this station again.

Mr. and Mrs. Walker have been here and seen the place, and can tell you plain. We give them when they asked us. We give a place for a sawmill up on one of our creeks, where there are plenty of trees. We saw it was for the good of our country, and we were all willing, but he had to go away before he finished it. So I, the king, write you myself to beg you to send us a missionary to teach us and our children God's way. We are begging God plenty for you to give us a missionary. Do come up to see us.

I am your friend and brother in Christ Jesus,
KING YESNO, of Bealoo Suke.

FOLK-LORE FROM AFRICA

(From the first native African baptized in Africa on the Congo, 1897.)

DEAR BISHOP HARTZELL: We left our country and came to Malange, and are staying with Mr. Gordon, who is very kind to us. We have had no school during these months. We are learning to speak Kimbundu. We are praying God to give you more missionaries to help our people here.

May the peace and love of our Lord Jesus Christ be with you! Your boy,

JOHN NWEBA.

DEAR BISHOP: I want to be a good worker for the Lord. I was a sinner first time, but Jesus has saved me from sin, and I praise Him. I have two sisters and two brothers that I want to be saved. Pray for them. I have been in school three years, and I am now about fifteen years old. I want to learn so that I can be useful to my people. All the boys and girls send love to you.

Your little friend,

LEWIS WAH.

"REDEEMED" GIRLS

Many of the good people in the home land question the system of redeeming or "buying" girls in Africa. Some of the missionaries, too, have doubted the wisdom of yielding that much to the heathen customs, but some good has resulted from this method, which was found to be absolutely necessary a few years ago. It is fast falling into disuse now, as our Christian natives bring their own children to the mission house. They do not want money for them. The custom is an old one, and it means nothing more nor less than that every native woman is expected to bring her parents a dowry. This sum ranges from twenty-five dollars to one hundred and fifty dollars, according to the prominence of the family, their prestige, and influence.

This sum is usually paid in cows, brass kettles, cloth, and beads. A cow, a brass kettle, and several pieces of cloth with several strings of beads is the usual price for an ordinary girl. When this amount has been given the parents, they no longer claim any jurisdiction over her. She is free from the parental law and must abide by the law of her purchaser; but as long as there is any part of the dowry unpaid, she is subject to her parents and may be called home at any time. The purchaser, however, has a right in such a case to demand of the parents what he has already paid, and they are compelled, according to their own laws, to give back this money, the purchaser thereby renouncing all his claim to the girl.

At one time it was impossible to get girls even for the mission without meeting this demand or living in dread of the parents taking the girls back to the heathen home whenever it pleased them. This was a very uncertain way to maintain a permanent work, and was very unsatisfactory; hence it became necessary to set these girls free if there was ever to be any hope for their advancement, and they were to become the Christian women of heathen Africa.

Among the girls who were thus ransomed from the bondage of heathenism years ago we can point with pride to many who now have Christian homes of their own, in which is established an altar of the living God. Many of these girls have gathered around them boys and girls from their heathen family and friends, and are training them according to the teachings and light they have received in the mission home, thus lifting up Christ in the midst of heathenism and gaining followers for His cause.

AFRICA'S HOPE LIES IN ITS YOUNG PEOPLE

A residence of a number of years in Liberia has afforded many a delightful opportunity of learning much of child and young life, of seeing them under varying circumstances, at work and at play, in Christian and heathen homes, in school and church; of sharing their laughing, fun, innocent amusements, merry sports, and observing their unfolding powers of body and mind.

Some years ago several little raw heathen chil-

MISSIONARY STORY SKETCHES

dren came from the interior of Liberia into our mission home. As I looked upon them they reminded me of unfledged birds that had fallen from the nest and strayed away from parental care. They had nothing to wear except strings of beads around their waists. Their toes were full of chiggers, and their little bodies covered with pimples; they were in a pitiable condition. They knew not a syllable of English, but it was interesting to hear their noisy babble and jabber in their native tongue, as they squatted at meals and at play. Within a few years they were altogether different children. Training of only a few years wrought a transformation that was simply marvelous; they could converse well in good English, read, write, cipher, sing, sew, sweep, dust, scrub, and perform with neat and excellent care many household duties.

In Krootown, a native village near Monrovia, the children are as numerous as bees in a hive. The town would be cheerless indeed without their noisy prattle and frolicsome maneuvers. It is always an interesting sight to watch them following a foreigner around the town, greeting him in their broken English, "How do, daddy; how do?" and offering their services to carry his luggage and to guide him to different parts of the town and vicinity. If the person has a camera, that gratifies their curiosity all the more, and they are ready

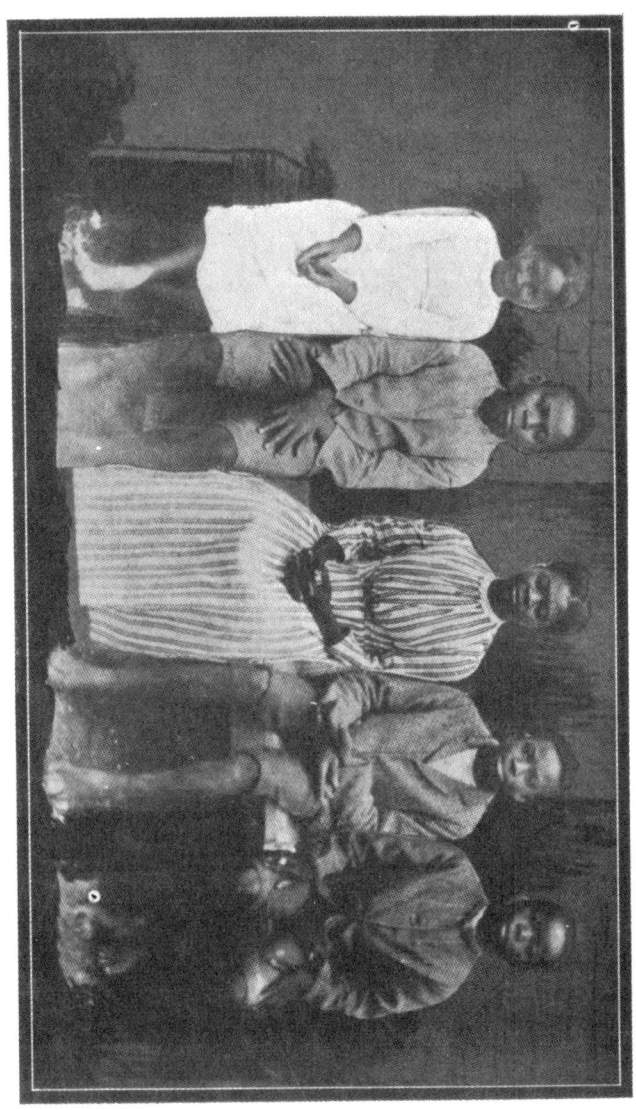

Our Young Hopefuls.

FOLK-LORE FROM AFRICA

at a moment's notice to pose for a picture, without the trouble of arranging toilet or position.

Children with such life as these free, happy youngsters have are usually bright and apt at books, so in our educational system we have arranged to admit them from the lowest grades on up to the more advanced classes, and they take to books with the same enthusiasm and success they show in their sports and fun. No department of our school work is more enjoyed by our teachers than the work among our "young hopefuls," and none holds out a more cheering sign of promise for Africa's uplift and redemption.

From the keen and lively interest our boys and girls take in school life, with its round of little duties and pleasures, and the progress they make in their lessons, one would never know the difference between them and the children born in civilization. When the school bell announces the noon hour, their little feet go "storming out to play." On the playground they are full of life and fun, enjoying such sports as ball, kite-flying, hoop-rolling, and wrestling. The African is light-hearted; he seems to possess by natural inheritance the gift of enjoying life, and nature helps him with her brilliant skies and abundant sunshine.

The story of one of their many happy days, July 26th, will give an idea of how they carry out their school exercises.

MISSIONARY STORY SKETCHES

It is Liberia's Independence Day—their "Glorious Twenty-sixth." Many little hearts beat with anxiety as they watch the cloud which hides the morning sun. When school time comes, the primary students, with their teachers, march from their little building with measured and even steps in double file to the school building. The walls echo a joyous chorus. This is followed by the reading of a psalm by a little girl of the third grade, and another chorus; members of the second and third grades recite gems of poetry, and a selection from "Liberia's National Fourth Reader" is given. "Liberia" is heartily sung. Then the teacher gives some facts about the Twenty-sixth of July, followed by impromptu remarks. After this a little girl standing in the south door waves the Liberian flag, as the school repeats:

"I pledge my allegiance to my flag,
And to the republic for which it stands,
One country, one flag, one nation indivisible."

The first chords of Liberia's national anthem sound on the organ as the pledge ends. The boys and girls join in singing the anthem, and file out of the schoolroom with a lively march. They have before them two weeks of vacation before the school bell calls again.

FOLK-LORE FROM AFRICA

A KROO BOY AND HIS CANOE

Kroo boys are experts in the use of their little canoes. It is always an interesting sight to watch with what ease and skill they propel their tiny boats on the sea. It matters not whether the waters are smooth or rough, they glide them as easily and swiftly as boys in other lands ride their bicycles on evenly asphalted streets.

Standing one day on the beach near Cape Mesurado, and watching the great swells of the sea dash against the rocks, I saw how a Kroo boy managed his canoe in the wild surf. He was some distance out at sea, but was making for the shore, with the bow of his boat quite out of the water. He was paddling industriously, his purpose being to take advantage of the approaching swells in their course, following each other in succession. His eyes were fixed upon a certain wave, which he knew would assist his effort. Therefore, with a dexterity that was commendable, he so adjusted his canoe and regulated his strokes that, mounting the desired swell, he was brought safe and dry to land.

Kroo men are well known in West Africa for their sea-faring life. Their acquaintance with the sea begins in youth and continues until they are well along in life. They have been called the Phœnicians of West Africa and are a hardy, stalwart race.

MISSIONARY STORY SKETCHES

LAND OF FLOWERS

Upon Bishop Isaiah B. Scott's first arrival in Liberia, soon after his election to the bishopric of Africa, a splendid reception was tendered him by the First Methodist Church, Monrovia. An appropriate program was tendered, composed of well-worded addresses and delightful music. Leading ministers and laymen of the city, as well as citizens generally, were present, filling the spacious church to its utmost capacity. A feature of the exercises was the presentation of a large bouquet of choice and fragrant roses.

In receiving the flowers the bishop said that he was agreeably surprised to find such beautiful objects as flowers in Liberia to admire, for the reverse of much that was attractive and charming had been related to him in connection with his going to Liberia on episcopal duties.

Liberia is a land of flowers. These differ from those of the temperate climes in brilliancy of color, luxuriancy of growth, and in emitting their odor only after sunset.

At the grave of Melville B. Cox, in Palm Grove Cemetery, is a frangipanni tree, exhaling its fragrance and casting its shade on the noted missionary's lowly bed.

A beautiful specimen of jessamine grows in the forest—

FOLK-LORE FROM AFRICA

" The flowers that wake while others sleep,
The timid jessamine buds that keep
Their fragrance to themselves all day;
But when the sunlight drives away,
Let their delicious secret out."

The oleander is a stately tree, twenty feet high. Its pink flowers are objects of beauty and richness. The lilies of the tropics are proverbial for delicacy and fragrance and beauty. The most remarkable is the chandelier lily, with its six petals four inches long, pending from beneath six stamens an inch shorter, growing out of the margin of a tunnel-shaped corolla. In the depth of the forest are flowers which emit a most delicate fragrance and are most pleasing to the eye.

While Africa is the "Dark Continent," so called, it is nevertheless the brightest on God's footstool, for there the Creator scatters sunshine with lavish hand and spreads His bounteous gifts everywhere. There flowers are always blooming and birds ever singing. Verily, the desert does "rejoice and blossom as the rose."

Dark but beautiful Africa made lovely by flowers, the smiles of God!

If nature can do so much in Africa in the making of flowers, what may we not expect of Nature's God to do for His own creatures there, who bear His image and likeness, and for whom He freely gave His only begotten Son to die?

MISSIONARY STORY SKETCHES

In Memoriam

AT A MARTYR'S GRAVE IN AFRICA

The first missionary of the Methodist Episcopal Church to Africa was Melville Beveridge Cox. He sleeps in Palm Grove Cemetery, Monrovia, and thus fills the first grave of the foreign missionary host of the Church.

The interest which centers around the grave of a martyr would naturally attract one to the resting place of the hero of Methodism in Africa.

As you approach the lot where the missionaries are interred and feel the cool breeze blowing from the south, and hear the murmurings of the restless waves dashing against the shore, strange emotions arise, and you instinctively feel that you are upon hallowed ground. You can not help but catch new inspiration from such sacred surroundings. Gazing upon the monument that marks the grave of the pioneer of these fallen heroes and heroines, you seem to hear again those immortal words of Cox, "Though a thousand fall, let not Africa be given up."

The brick wall which surrounds the lot has crumbled here and there, suggesting the perishable decay of man and the work of his hand; but nature has spread a soft blanket of verdure over these unsightly places, which completely hides the bricks grown dark with age. A modest frangi-

FOLK-LORE FROM AFRICA

panni shrub stands blooming near, shedding its fragrance afar. The grave is marked by a white marble monument eight feet in height, consisting of a freestone base, surmounted by an obelisk. The entire monument has grown dark beneath the glare of the tropical sun and pelting rains. On one side, facing the north, is the following inscription:

To the memory of the
REV. MELVILLE B. COX,
the first missionary from the Methodist Episcopal Church in the U. S. to Liberia, W. A. He arrived in Monrovia on the 9th of March, 1833, where, having organized a branch of the same Church, he died in the triumphs of the Christian faith on the 21st of July of the same year. Aged 34 years.

He sleeps on the palm-fringed shores of Africa, but his influence abides, and many since his death have caught his heroic spirit and have borne the standard he first unfurled in the "Dark Continent." Some, like him, have laid their lives on Africa's altar, a sacrifice to God; to which fact the row of graves of deceased missionaries testifies more eloquently than words.

"Being dead, he yet speaketh," for the foundations of Methodism, which he laid, remain an everlasting memorial and bear witness to the inestimable good which he so heroically wrought.

A PRAYER

We thank Thee, O God, for the opportunity Thou didst give us to study and labor in Africa. We thank Thee for those with whom we were associated in Christian work and for personal contact there with the natives, both Christian and heathen. We pray that Thou wouldst abundantly bless the labors of the missionaries in that field and the respective societies under whose auspices they work. Sustain their courage, increase their zeal, quicken their devotion, deepen their conviction of duty, fortify them by principles of uprightness, and make them a positive blessing among the people. We pray that Thou wouldst equip them by Thy might for the warfare against the powers of darkness, and may their triumph be sure and glorious.

Bless the native converts. Establish them in the faith, and grant that under the direction and tutelage of the Holy Spirit they may daily increase in knowledge and in the strength of God.

Bless and prosper every agency—political, commercial, industrial, and missionary—employed for Africa's awakening and redemption, and hasten

A PRAYER

the glad day when Africa shall cease to be the "Dark Continent," and when no longer shrouded in darkness and degradation it shall rise and shine in the light of the glory of God.

We pray that Thou wouldst with loving favor and tenderest compassion bless the Republic of Liberia, that distant outpost on the west coast of Africa representing the civilization of the American Negro and his descendants on his ancestral soil. Let Thy benediction rest upon her continually. Disperse the troubles that threaten and disturb her, and usher in the dawn of a better and more auspicious day.

Strengthen the bond of sympathy between the people of this country and Liberia, an offshoot of this great Republic, to whom we are debtors. Help us to speedily recognize our obligation to her. May we in this relation rise to the largest measure of Christian duty.

We pray for the pagan tribes of Liberia dwelling in the uplands and uninvaded fastnesses of the jungles, who in this day of grace are still unreached by the gospel of Jesus Christ. Hasten, O hasten to them the glorious message of salvation and the blessings of civilization, and through them may the savage tribes in the regions beyond be speedily reached!

Let Thy blessings rest upon all the Churches and denominations laboring in Liberia. May Chris-

A PRAYER

tianity in the Republic be virile, spiritual, and aggressive, and its advocates supremely loyal to Jesus Christ, that in all things He might have the preeminence.

We pray that Thou, O Lord, wouldst advance and prosper the work of the Methodist Episcopal Church in Africa. Bless Thy servants Bishop Hartzell and Bishop Scott, whom the Church has ordained and consecrated to that special work and upon whom is placed the responsibility of supervision and leadership there.

Endow them with wisdom and understanding adequate for their great work, and make them by Thy grace eminent in service and successful. May the sacred interests committed to their keeping be ever safe and secure. Shield and protect them from the perils of sea and land in their long journeys in supervising the work of God on the continent. Strengthen them for their difficult task, and may their health and lives be ever precious in Thy sight.

We pray that in this year of Jubilee for Africa there may be felt throughout our world-wide Methodism an interest commensurate with the needs of the field, and the redemption of the continent hastened.

Hear us, O God, we humbly beseech Thee, in the name of Jesus Christ, to whom, with the Father and Holy Spirit, shall be unceasing praise! Amen.